Mid-Career Change Series, Volume 2

RELAUNCH!

*Stagnation, Change, and Renewal
in Mid-Career and Beyond*

Steven Simon, Ph.D.

RELAUNCH! Stagnation, Change, and Renewal in Mid-Career and Beyond

Second Edition

Published by
DocUmeant Publishing
244 5th Avenue, Suite G-200
NY, NY 10001

646-233-4366

Editor: Eileen Spiegler

Technical Editor and Advisor: Tennyson J. Wright, Ph.D., CRC

Cover Design & Formatting: DocUmeant Designs
DocUmeantDesigns.com

Publisher's Cataloging-In-Publication Data
(Prepared by The Donohue Group, Inc.)

Names: Simon, Steven E., author.
Title: Relaunch! : stagnation, change, and renewal in mid-career and beyond / Steven Simon, Ph.D.
Description: First edition. | NY, NY : DocUmeant Publishing, 2018. | Series: Mid-career change series ; volume 2 | Includes index.
Identifiers: ISBN 9781937801960;
    Library of Congress Control Number: 2018962687
Subjects: LCSH: Job satisfaction. | Work--Psychological aspects. | Middle age--Psychological aspects. | Career changes.
Classification: LCC HF5549.5.J63 S56 2018 | DDC 658.3/1422--dc23

First edition. March 15, 2018. First Printing. March 15, 2018

Contents

Foreword

Work is one of the most important activities for people throughout the world. Work bestows a sense of importance! Work embodies a sense of value and connectedness to others. Work provides something to do and a place to go every day. Whether you're working to support your family, to provide a second income for your family, or to engage in social activity, work is essential to your health and well-being.

Many of us seek the most satisfying work based on factors such as interests, aptitudes, education, personality, environmental fit, emotions, and opportunity, among other things. Some of us rely on chance while others choose a more systematic approach to find their ideal job or career. While experts and career theorists may differ on the approach, all agree that finding a job that satisfies one's basic needs is the goal. Whether we spend one year or 30 years in a job or career, we want our work to be satisfying, challenging, and sufficient to support our basic needs of food, clothing and shelter.

So, what happens when you lose your job due to something that is completely beyond your control such as a layoff, a sudden and unexpected illness, a change in management or the death of your spouse that results in the loss of income or benefits? What happens if you experience stagnation or general loss of interest in what you're doing at work? Or perhaps you're seeking a more exciting line of work or more income and job satisfaction. Or, maybe you're seeking renewal or a second career! These situations suggest a need for change in order to establish or renew a sense of meaning and satisfaction in work. Whatever the reason or reasons, it's important to take charge and responsibility by seeking guidance and support from professionals, and reading guides that are practical and user friendly.

Dr. Steven Simon, a leading career expert, provides clear and common approaches to achieving a satisfying and productive job or career change by responding to those questions and issues and many more in *RELAUNCH! Stagnation, Change, and Renewal in Mid-Career and Beyond. RELAUNCH!* offers antidotes to stagnating in a job or career and offers ways to create passion in your work. Furthermore, it offers practical solutions to address real-life issues. Dr. Simon has done a magnificent job of blending blogs he has authored over several years, along with new chapters he has co-authored with other professionals, into a cogent and practical resource.

Dr. Simon joins an elite field of career experts who provide useful and practical information to address job and career questions that people like you face every day. Will you be one of the millions of people who change jobs one or more times in their lifetime? Despite the fuzzy definitions and differences among career experts and the U.S. Department of Labor as to what constitutes a "job change" verses a "career change", there is little disagreement that millions of people will change their place of employment and field of employment several times in their lifetime. In addition, the frequency of change differs between populations such as baby boomers, millennials, males, females, socio-economic groups, races, those with different levels of educational achievement, and the like. Career experts such as Alison Doyle (https://tinyurl.com/yc6725b4) estimate that the average person changes jobs 10–15 times during his or her career. Simon Davies (https://tinyurl.com/yafpcs58) reports that the average person will change careers 5–7 times during their working life. Likely, you will be one of these individuals in your lifetime.

What can you do to make your transition from one job or career easier and more productive? What can you do to find the job or career that ignites or reignites a sense of passion and meaning in what you do? That's easy to answer! *RELAUNCH!* It's a must read for anyone who is, has, or will be experiencing stagnation, and wishes to make the *change* needed to achieve renewal *in mid-career and beyond!*

Tennyson J. Wright, Ph.D., CRC
Associate Professor Emeritus
Former Chair, Department of Rehabilitation & Mental Health Counseling
Former Interim Director, School of Social Work
Former Vice Provost, Academic Affairs
University of South Florida
Tampa, FL
January 2018

Acknowledgments

I'd like to thank those who have helped so much in putting this book together.

Eileen Spiegler, my editor, spent hours providing content editing and general journalistic advice. Eileen is a former long-term news editor and writer for one of the country's largest newspapers. As the newspaper industry dwindled, she has had several writing jobs and continues to try to find her "passion" in academic, arts, or journalistic writing. What a superbly skilled and talented person!

Dr. Tennyson J. Wright, served in the role of technical editor and advisor. With his knowledge of the career field, he provided the essential editing and advice for content accuracy, adequate explanation, illustration, and conceptual clarity of technical information. Tennyson is a valued colleague, and recently retired Associate Professor and Chair of the Department of Rehabilitation and Mental Health Counseling at the University of South Florida. He previously served as Vice-Provost, Academic Affairs, as well as Interim Director of the School of Social Work. He is a widely respected national figure in his field and has published and edited extensively. He is also the author of the Foreword to this book. I greatly appreciate the time and work he put into this project, and particularly the essential advice he provided.

Bonnie Simon played a prominent role in synthesis of the intersection principle, a straightforward way of summarizing what I'd observed and known for years about how people find passion and meaning in their work. When she described in detail her own observations in corporate America and from the hundreds of interviews she's done with small business owners, what I had been observing all came together into an easily communicated principle. Much of the book builds on that principle. You will read about it in Chapter 7, which Bonnie and I co-authored. Bonnie is also a superb writer, who taught me about her very effective and folksy "on the porch" writing style.

Fernando Narvaez played an instrumental role in the book, both in writing and as a legal consultant. He was a co-author of Chapter 5, in which he introduced the concept of the "paradigm of ourselves."

It's based on observations during his years of experience as a Social Security attorney that clients with disabilities have difficulty changing careers because of the pre-disability work image they have of themselves. He also co-authored three of the four chapters in Part 7 of the book, all based on the concepts in blog articles on disability that we published together. Fernando also was of great help with legal issues associated with publishing of the book.

Dr. Jeffrey Diamond, my long-term friend and colleague, did a detailed read of the final manuscript for consistency, flow, and anything else we all missed or forgot about. He was amazing, proving that editing never ends! Jeff spent his career in school guidance, thus having expertise in career, education, and counseling issues. He was most recently a Director of Guidance for the Fauquier County Public School System in Virginia.

Elise Prezant started out as a reader of the manuscript. Then, her astute observations led to adding a separate (co-authored) chapter on age. I am so grateful for her picking up on things I didn't emphasize enough. Elise has managed and provided career and vocational rehabilitation services to mid- and late career clients over the past 25 years at several community organizations in New Jersey and Atlanta, Georgia. She is currently a career counselor and project director for the Jewish Family Service in Somerville, New Jersey.

I would also like to acknowledge the contributions of my wife, Gail Simon, who read the manuscript, made "gentle" constructive criticisms, and put up with all the time I spent writing this book. She also gets credit for any writing skills I learned. With her education background, when we were still in college, she read my papers and taught me how to turn a half page run-on sentence into something understandable!

Thanks to Kimberly Williams, my assistant, who spent numerous hours formatting and reformatting draft after draft of my two books over the past year. I am grateful for her skills and patience with me in doing this and all the other thankless things she has learned, to help me publish while keeping the rest of the business running. Thanks also go to Vivian Greene who carefully did the final grammatical manuscript edit.

I also wish to thank and acknowledge all those who contributed with the real stories of mid-career challenges, struggles, and triumphs I've heard directly and through case records I have reviewed. Making this book relevant, practical, and useful for readers would not have been possible otherwise.

Finally, a special thanks goes to my son Matt Simon, a mid-career professional himself whose ability to listen and provide insight from his work in organization consulting and his own career development has always been extremely helpful.

Introduction

RELAUNCH! is different.

Reading *RELAUNCH!* is not like the articles, blogs, and lists of solutions to career problems "10 Ways to . . ." that constantly inundate us on social media sites, in our spam folders, and on bookstore shelves. *RELAUNCH!* did develop out of a series of blog articles I wrote alone or jointly. However, they were all written with the underlying theme of successively addressing the most salient issues encountered in mid- and late career that impede performing meaningful and satisfying work. The goal was to help readers who followed these articles to turn that around. Over 100,000 readers found and viewed the articles on the internet. Most have now been removed to make way for a complete updating and organizing of the material for the book.

As the full title implies, *RELAUNCH!* is about the antidotes to stagnating in a job or career you don't love or even like or find boring day in and day out. It's also about creating passion for and meaning in work when you choose to or must transition from what you were previously doing.

Why is this important? According to a recent comprehensive report, employees spend 54% of their waking hours working.[1] For a full-time professional, when we factor in commuting time and even thinking about the job, it's reasonable to conclude that a higher figure is more typical. If you are a business owner or organization leader, the percentage is likely to be even higher.

Many of you know this from your experience. You also know that if you dislike or feel little meaning for what you do or where you do it, you open yourself to excessive negative stress and give up the opportunity for a far more enriched and mentally healthier life. Wouldn't it be great to wake up on Monday morning and think "I can't wait to get to work" rather than "only five days till the weekend"?

---

1   CoreNet Global and Solexo, LLC (2014). The Workplace Experience© Survey. Thought Leadership App. Retrieved from http://itunes.apple.com

RELAUNCH! also differentiates itself from other career self-help books by addressing real-life issues of those who have been working for many years, and who long for and hope to work with a passion for the rest of their careers. The issues are based on my nearly 50 years of experience as a career counselor, vocational expert, and counseling psychologist, academically trained in the career field, who has listened to the stories of and viewed the job histories of over 15,000 individuals, mostly at some stage of mid- or late career.

RELAUNCH! zeros in on themes I have seen frequently and as most significant to renewing a sense of passion and meaning for work once stagnation has set in, or when a new phase of life is about to begin. Although it is not inclusive of every issue one might experience, it summarizes and integrates my observations of those that are most related to strong perceptions of a need for change.

An important part of the book is providing tools and strategies to bring about the change needed to renew and find new passion and meaning in work. Some of the strategies involve major life change, while others require simple adjustments. In many of the chapters, links are provided to additional resources to assist with carrying out a strategy. In some, there are instructions and worksheets for doing self-assessments. Resources for outside help when needed and cost-free when possible, are provided throughout the book as well. If you've purchased the electronic version, you will be able to link directly to much of this information.

As an academically trained careerist, I must point out that this book is not an "academic" work, nor would it meet academic standards for research or its writing approach. It is meant it to be a "practical" book, easy to read, understand, and apply to your experience. It is based on the academic knowledge that I've assimilated, combined with my experience in helping others with career issues.

You'll also notice that I often write in the first person, including in co-authored chapters, to best express my or our perceptions, observations, and experiences, to you as readers. Think of it as our sitting on your porch, where we're informally talking about these things.

So, if you are roughly 10, 20 or more years into a career, are struggling with various forms of dissatisfaction, and feel a gnawing need for change in the work sector of your life, you will relate to the content of this book. By this time, you have been working long enough to decide whether this is the path you want to be on longer term, or if you think you need an injection of passion and meaning in what you do on a day-to-day basis.

Similarly, you may be ready to retire and don't want to stop working, or you may be grappling with how to deal with illness or disability while maintaining a meaningful job and income. *RELAUNCH!* should help you understand what you want, help you assess your willingness and tolerance for change, and show you what you can do and how to do what is needed to relaunch your life toward a renewed or newly created sense of passion for and meaning in your work.

Steven Simon, Ph. D.

PART 1

Stagnation, Change, and Renewal

Stagnation is a loss of interest in being productive and in improving oneself. It is the antithesis of feeling a sense of passion and meaning from one's work.

When are you in stagnation? How did you get there, and more importantly how do you get out or avoid it altogether and break through to career renewal? The following chapters overview and look at real situations involving the stagnation, change, and renewal process.

CHAPTER 1

Stagnation

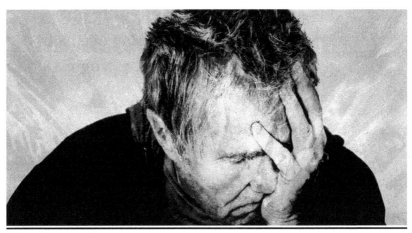

Photo by typographyimages

Bill's Going Nowhere . . . And You?

Bill is a computer support specialist in a large company. He helps employees manage hardware and software problems. He had some college, but "fell" into this occupation when he had to work while going to school. Now in his mid-40s with a wife, two teenagers, and a home, he has never completed formal training, and feels stuck. He's not keeping up with rapidly changing technology and doesn't even like what he's doing. He's bored and says "I feel like I'm going nowhere in this career and I can't see things changing. At this point I hate going to work." Bill believes he ended up in the wrong field and is now paying the price.

If you're in the middle or late in your career, you may be feeling tired of or bored with your job. Everyone feels this way sometimes, but for you, this has been going on pretty much day in and day out.

You may commiserate with family or colleagues about how terrible things are. You may even be counting years and days to retirement.

Or, you may feel like you're not accomplishing anything meaningful, maybe like you're overwhelmed, yet just spinning your wheels. You may be angry, depressed, or feeling anxious about going to work. You're not even getting much feedback about how well you're doing from your boss, co-workers or clients, reinforcing the feeling that what you do doesn't matter very much and that you're going nowhere in your career.

The symptoms of stagnation can insidiously build and intensify unless something occurs to break the progression.

You may have had a series of unsuccessful jobs and are now unemployed. Maybe you've moved to different unsatisfying jobs due to necessity; that is, having to get some job, any job, after layoffs or terminations. Regardless of the reasons, you're certainly not feeling any excitement about the work you do. Rather than looking forward to it, you look forward to getting away from it.

This is what stagnation feels like. Some of those who have contacted me for career consulting have literally been at the point of screaming if they had to go back to work for another day. Maybe you feel or have felt that way.

Stagnation usually builds over time. For example, we enter a career, find a job or maybe move through several jobs. There's excitement and achievement early on, but either that declines or stops as routine sets in. If nothing changes to rekindle interest, then eventually stagnation starts to take hold.

However, even while the stage is being set for long-term stagnation, we can also be getting more entrenched in a career or job and an organization. While we are working hard to succeed, salary and benefits increase, and lifestyle changes follow. This build-up often takes place during a period when family responsibilities and expenses are increasing. So, we start to become locked into a path that brings with it a desired lifestyle and the means to support it. As with Bill, often that includes failing to develop skills beyond the immediate job or seeking new opportunities. When we remain in this type of static job situation the symptoms of stagnation can insidiously build and intensify unless something occurs to break the progression.

Stagnation and Life Transitions

In some instances, stagnation may or may not be in progress, but circumstances make the chances high in the near future unless action is taken quickly. For example, some of us will experience illness or disability at some point in our careers, serious enough that we can no longer do the work we were doing, perform at a diminished level, or not at all. Then what? Resulting life transitions, including the need for a less demanding job, can present special challenges with potential to precipitate a downward spiral.

Janelle, a registered nurse, has worked in hospitals for 38 years. She has advanced to a head nurse position and is not in a stagnating mode. In fact, she loves her work and is widely respected by her patients and colleagues. She's not ready to retire anytime soon. However, she has a back condition that has worsened to the point that she will soon no longer be able to provide direct patient care.

She saw this coming for years but did not plan for a job or career change. There are no other less strenuous nursing jobs for her at the hospital. When Janelle leaves her job (or is forced to leave), her challenge will be to find another job or career that maintains or renews her love of what she does and that she is physically able to do. If she doesn't make the right choices, she could end up quickly moving toward stagnation.

If you are retiring from a full-time career or job, and choose to continue working part-time in retirement, you could face the impact of stagnation as well. Robert, the vice-president of sales for a medium-sized wholesale jewelry business was preparing to retire at the mandatory age of 68. He didn't want to retire but was forced by company policy to do so. However, the company retained him on a contract basis to do some part-time sales in retirement, allowing him to continue relationships with former accounts he knew. This, at least partially, gave him the opportunity to ease into his transition by continuing in an activity he enjoyed. Although he no longer had the control and status of the vice president job, significant career stagnation was avoided while he worked through the change to a retirement lifestyle. Had he been forced to take an unrelated job when he wasn't ready to stop working, or simply stopped working with nothing drawing him to retirement, stagnation might have progressed rapidly.

So, as in Bill's case, stagnation can be insidious, creeping up with slowly developing loss of work interest and the accompanying downward emotional spiral. The questions then become, how can we execute the changes needed to reverse it? Or better yet, how can we make pre-emptive changes to avoid stagnation and facilitate ongoing renewal before stagnation has the chance to begin?

When major life transitions precipitate a job or career change without readiness like through disability or retirement, stagnation can come on quickly due to withdrawal from a crucial source of life satisfaction. In these cases, anticipating and planning in advance is important. This was possible in Janelle's and Robert's cases. Janelle hasn't done that yet, but she still has a window of opportunity. Robert planned with the help of his company and was able to arrange for a meaningful transitional job.

In summary, stagnation can take the passion and meaning out of a job you have now, or from a new job that follows a life transition when lost satisfaction cannot be replaced. The goal is to reverse the stagnation process or prevent it from happening at all.

CHAPTER 2

Change and Renewal

Photo by Alexas_Fotos

Andrea the Renewer

A ndrea is a 68-year-old retired teacher. She completed a bachelor's degree in secondary education with a minor in library science in her early 20s and worked as a school librarian for three years. Then, while her children were growing up, she did part-time substitute teaching for eight years until she began working full-time as a high school teacher. Throughout her work life, she took continuing education courses, completed a master's degree in special education, and a certificate program in brain-based education.

At age 52, due to her excellent background in education and ability to relate well to special needs students, she was invited to be the assigned teacher in a community drug treatment program for teenage offenders. She loved this new job and continued to take workshops and courses, this time in alcohol and drug treatment. She finally retired at 66, mainly because her health did not allow for the rigors of high energy, full-time work.

The best way to avoid stagnation is not to get there in the first place! But it goes further than that. We are looking not only for avoidance of stagnation, but for active renewal.

However, she was offered a job to run groups one night a week in an after-school program for high schoolers caught using drugs at school, and their parents. This allowed her to continue to experience the passion she always had for her work, while leaving the opportunity to tend to her health needs and spend more time with her grandchildren.

As we can see with Andrea, the best way to avoid stagnation is not to get there in the first place! But it goes further than that. We are looking not only for avoidance of stagnation, but for active renewal, the growth and development that helps us move toward a continuing sense of passion for, and meaning in, whatever work we do . . . exactly what Andrea achieved.

Something Always Needs to Change

Achieving passion and meaning is not a static state. With Andrea, her career was dynamic. Nothing remained the same for too long. And her actions over time were proactive to avoid future stagnation and maintain active renewal.

So, even if you're feeling great about your job this year or today, that could change next year or tomorrow. If your job remains the same and you remain the same, over time *you will stagnate*. Something always needs to change for renewal to take place.

The Role of Chance

Although we know that being proactive can help, chance also plays a role in how life unfolds. Sometimes circumstances change, such as an unexpected job opportunity, a company reorganization, a layoff that leads to an unexpected business opportunity, assignment to a new, high-profile project, or an illness or disability. Sometimes we meet someone new or lose someone which changes the course of our life. We cannot control the occurrences or when they happen. However, we can proactively control the preparation we do over time to take advantage of chance when it comes along. Andrea took courses, got an advanced degree, and always sought new career experiences. Her pattern of ongoing development put her in position to later take advantage of chance opportunities in the substance abuse treatment field that led to further change and renewal.

Larry Digs Out

Larry, a state government executive, came to me at age 58, uncertain whether to remain an assistant in his agency or seek a directorship elsewhere. He had lost all interest in what he was doing since the work and level of responsibility had become so routine. Becoming a director would involve major changes, including a possible geographical move, plus adjusting to a new work setting.

Although he would have more status and responsibility as a director, he was quite comfortable in his current agency, was well-liked, and had excellent community ties. A more limited change option was to ask his current director for assignment to run an important long-term community development project. He made that choice, planned how he would approach his director, and his request was approved.

This assignment created a new, exciting dimension to his job and a sense that he could contribute something very meaningful to his community if the project was successful. In this case, a minimal change strategy was enough to create the conditions for renewing job passion and meaningfulness.

If you're already experiencing stagnation as Larry was, it may be time to "dig out." Or, if you are or are not experiencing stagnation and are about to make a transition, perhaps due to disability or retirement, it's time to act to avoid a stagnating experience and assure a renewal. You can't reliably depend on being rescued by chance, just as you can't reliably depend on winning the lottery.

Digging out and life transitioning involves deciding how much change and the types of change you're willing and able to make; your change tolerance. You must decide what changes you want to make; plan them; and execute the plan. Finally, deciding how to make change an ongoing and proactive part of your work lifestyle can help avoid significant future stagnation.

The Challenges of Change

Sometimes, the decisions around making a change are the biggest challenges in moving forward to renewal. For example, we may be thinking about a change, but are we really committed to it?

We all dream about some ideal, like starting our own business and not answering to a "clueless" boss. But, are we committed enough to think "I'll do everything I need to do to get there. I'm ready." Then, once we make the mental commitment, can we initiate it and do it? There's a difference between thinking and doing. Anyone who's made a New Year's resolution can attest to that!

Then there's the extent of change. How much change can we tolerate? Larry could not easily tolerate a major job change and moving far away. Thus, mental commitment and execution of change was much more feasible when it required limited upheaval and risk.

Finally, the ability to make a change is contingent on our ability to see ourselves in a new role. This is a psychological transition that involves how we see ourselves and how others see us. We have observed that sometimes what seems to be even a simple change from one occupation to another can be impeded by an identity issue.

In Chapter 5, we give the example of a client, a long-time truck driver, who could not conceive of making a necessary career change due to disability, because he always saw himself as a truck driver. No matter what your long-term career happens to be, if you experience this feeling when envisioning a change, you're not alone.

The above are all issues we've heard from mid- and late-career clients that have impacted whether change is feasible. These issues and how to successfully manage them at various career stages are dealt with in detail in Part 2.

So, in summary, to find renewal, change of some type is always needed. However, the challenges around making changes are often the most formidable barriers to overcome.

Photo by Geralt

PART 2
The Paradox of Career Change

Change is the most critical factor in reversing or preventing stagnation. If you can't make some type of change, you reduce your chances of turning things around or preventing a downward spiral. Changes can be major, such as a complete change in career or a life upending job change; or they can be on a smaller scale, like acquiring new skills or changing work assignments on your current job.

We often recognize a need to make a career adjustment, sometimes a desperate need, but the result never materializes. This is the paradox of career change: wanting to do it and perhaps making some degree of commitment, but not choosing or being able to follow through.

The chapters that follow explore issues related to the paradox of career change and how to manage them.[2]

---

2   The most successful approach for managing change discussed in most of these chapters is consistent with the change process theory of German-American social psychologist Kurt Lewin.

CHAPTER 3

Are You Really Ready to Commit to Major Change?

Photo by RobinHiggins

Edward is Locked-In

Edward is a psychologist working for the federal prison system. He has had this job for 20 years and is now in his mid-40s. As a federal worker, he has excellent health benefits at relatively low cost, a solid retirement plan, and more vacation and sick time than he can use. He had a bout with early prostate cancer but has had no recurrence in the past six years. His job has been stable, he is at a high pay grade, and thus is assured of a good salary until he retires. His wife works as a physician and their income supports a home in a high-end neighborhood, private schools for the kids, and pretty much everything else they want or need.

Unfortunately, he no longer gets much satisfaction from his job. It's very routine, the professional challenges are limited, and he has few other colleagues with whom to share work experiences. It's so boring that he has caught himself falling asleep some days. At other times, he gets so frustrated that he loses his temper easily with his boss and sometimes, inappropriately, with clients. However, he knows he can coast to retirement in 10 years. He won't get fired.

Edward has explored other possibilities, such as a full-time faculty or research job at a university, and opportunities in a private group practice. But, he can't commit to change. He's locked into the federal system. What happens if he loses his insurance and the cancer comes back? Will another employer offer as good a medical plan as the one he has? What happens if he loses that job? If he needed to get private insurance, how much would that cost? Maybe it won't even be available in the future due to his pre-existing condition. Then there's the issue of salary. He's almost guaranteed to stay at his high salary now. If he leaves he might have to start lower or lose stability if he doesn't do well in the new job. What about potential loss of some retirement benefits if he goes elsewhere?

If you are a professional in the middle third of your career, like Edward, at some point you've probably considered making a significant career or job shift. If you are in a stagnation pattern or in a downward career trajectory, the urgency to make a big change may seem even greater.

Conflicting Factors

Easier said (or thought) than done, right? In my experience, two major conflicting factors often emerge for those who have been in a relatively uninterrupted early career pattern, and particularly those in mid-life, roughly late 30s to early 50s. First, there may be a nagging desire to try a more satisfactory career path before it's too late, but second, there is realization of the financial realities of making a change. Time becomes particularly important because the deeper you get into a job, employer, or career, the more "locked in" you may feel (or be).

Sometimes the grass looks greener elsewhere, but major work change may not be the answer.

Change often means the possibility of salary or other economic loss at a time you and your family can least afford it. You may have accrued benefits, have health insurance that might not be duplicated elsewhere, or have promotion/partnership possibilities. You don't want to see financial growth regress or be interrupted. Yet at the same time, the longer you stay put, the less you perceive you will ever be able to make a change.

Six Critical Areas to Consider

As you grapple with the "two major conflicting factors", consider the following six key areas in deciding whether to embark on a major change:

1. **How important is a change?** Maybe you have strong interest in or passion for another type of work. The reasons we enter a career may have little relationship to how we view our choice after being in the career for 10 or 20 years. Perhaps you want to break out of a stressful work pattern or a stifling work environment. Maybe you are unchallenged, or conversely, can never meet expectations and have lost confidence in your capabilities. Whatever the reasons, do you no longer look forward to going to work, see no better future, feel gnawing anxiety about your situation, or ask yourself, "is this all there is for me?" In effect, how deeply are you entrenched in this type of stagnation and how badly do you want to get out?

2. **Is a change of job or career going to improve your life?** Will it bring back the sense of passion and meaning you are missing? Sometimes the grass looks greener elsewhere, but major work change may not be the answer. The same issues may pop up in another workplace or career. Maybe internal (self) change or adjustments in other aspects of your life are needed. Emotional

issues that interfere with overall life satisfaction can impact any job or career. What you can do to improve coping and perhaps avoid the need for major career change is covered in Chapters 29 and 30. It's important to do some honest introspection about what brings you to the point of feeling the need for a job or career change. Sometimes talking this out with a counselor can help objectively clarify the situation.

3. **Do you have the financial resources and temperament to take on the risks of a change?** Some changes are lower risk, such as finding a better job in your field. Others, such as starting a new career or your own business can be high risk. For example, if you are a corporate executive and decide to become an art dealer, you would need to be able to tolerate substantial risk of failure and/or have financial resources that you are willing to use. All career changes involve some risk, and if you want to maintain financial stability, *having financial reserves is important.* Also, if you fail or see failure coming, will you have the emotional stamina to bounce back quickly?

4. **What is your stress tolerance?** The change process itself can be stressful since there are many unknowns. Don't underestimate the impact of a major change on family and others close to you. If you have a spouse or significant other, how much support will they provide? Do you have major childcare or other family responsibilities? Depending upon the nature of the change, you will experience some upheaval. Will the short-term consequences of negative stress outweigh the stress of staying put? If the change doesn't work out, there could be high stress over the long-term. But, if at the end of the tunnel yours and others quality of life is measurably improved, the stress in getting there will be worth it.

5. **How is your health?** If you or your family has health or disability issues, costs and adequacy of insurance should be considered before and beyond the decision to make a change. On the other hand, if illness or disability is responsible for problems with your work, carefully planned change may be the best choice. For example, if you are a sales representative who has chronic disabling panic attacks precipitated by the competitive stress of sales quotas, you're likely going to need a change to a different field of work—the sooner the better!

6. **Are you ready to invest in new learning?** Have you kept up with your industry and profession? Changes for the better usually involve studying, learning unfamiliar information, and adjusting to contemporary ways of doing things. You may need to take courses, workshops, and learn new practices and technology. It may also be necessary to get a new degree and certifications.

In summary, a realistic decision about major mid- to late career change may come down to resolving the conflict between wishes and reality. Readiness can be determined by assessing your perception of the potential benefits, your risk and stress tolerances, and your willingness and ability to do what is necessary to effect successful change.

How would you assess the reality of Edward's committing to a major job change? Do you think he should do it, or opt for another way of managing his stagnation?

Photo by ID 97318901 © Halifah Rahmansyah | Dreamstime.com

CHAPTER 4

Commitment is One Thing: Doing It Is Something Else

Don's and Jim's Resistance to Change

Don, a successful New York personal injury lawyer, finally decided it's time to take the plunge and become a bed and breakfast owner. He had just about had it with the depositions, hard negotiations, and contentious court battles, and he had the resources to make the change to what he really wanted to do. He met all the criteria for that commitment. But, when it came to taking action to close the law practice and get ready to sign the contract for the B and B in New Hampshire, he discovered that doing it is another story. He couldn't do it.

At mid- or late career, even with a sense of readiness, the psychological phenomenon of resistance to change can quickly kick in. As ready as we seem and as much as we feel a need to make a change, there's something that tells us "better the devil you know than the devil you don't," or quite simply, *we fear the unknown.* Some of this thinking is realistic and prevents reckless, stressful, and potentially poor decision-making. However, it can also prevent us from breaking out of a dysfunctional psychological box.

A few more examples of recent career situations I've encountered come to mind.

Jim is a 51-year-old emergency medicine physician, highly stressed in his work. As a dedicated, patient-centered doctor, he's been disillusioned with the quality of service delivery in hospitals and facilities for which he's worked most of his career, and the medical establishment in general. He is deeply disturbed by every medical error he observes and feels no sense of control in how he believes things should be done. He feels overly stressed and would like to leave the practice of medicine. In fact, he thinks he never should have entered the field.

He needed heart surgery this year, which now leaves him with other chronic stressors in his life, including the costs of his own medical care. With employer benefits, his medical co-pays after surgery were more than his family could afford, and he needs continuing care. He says he wants to change careers, but when it comes down to considering the alternatives, he rejects the options and opts to continue, unhappy and stressed, with what he has. His commitment to changing careers is stated, but, in reality, mild at best.

> **As much as we feel a need to make a change, there's something that tells us "better the devil you know than the devil you don't," or quite simply, we fear the unknown.**

Analyzing Jim's situation, his resistance to changing careers stems from his deep investment in becoming a doctor, developing as a physician in his specialty, and his underlying belief that he will never find another career that will satisfy his financial needs. Not only that, being a physician is a major part of his identity. Changing to another career would undermine this "self-paradigm," which includes his self-esteem and social status. So even when considering opportunities for more compatible physician jobs, including those that might provide medical insurance, he rejects the change options. Due to unwillingness to make even a low-risk transition, Jim places himself in the position of seeing no hope in sight with continuing dissatisfaction and stress, and perhaps life-threatening medical risk.

Breaking Through Barriers to Change

Breaking through barriers to change is complex and the reasons differ from person to person. But fear of change or of the unknown, particularly with respect to possible loss of income, is a common underlying theme.

Julia is a financially successful 58-year-old certified public accountant in private practice. She is well respected by her clients and peers and has had a niche practice for over 30 years. She is comfortable and financially secure, but bored. She thinks maybe she still has time to make a change to something that would make a meaningful social contribution and rejuvenate her life. However, after discussing it with a career counselor and considering the options, she decides to stay where she is.

Julia's situation is in sharp contrast to Jim's. While Jim is experiencing acute distress from which he finds no escape, Julia is neither highly-stressed nor deeply dissatisfied. Her interest in changing careers is most related to a desire for new growth and development. While she too is resistant to acting on a total career change because she fears loss of income, changing careers right away is not an urgent concern.

Julia is interested in trying new alternatives, such as teaching disadvantaged children. Through part-time education, volunteering, and later some paid teaching work, she could eventually transition into this second career as she approaches financially comfortable retirement as an accountant. Resistance to total change at this point is a functional choice for Julia while she explores other possibilities for a gradual transition within the next 5–10 years. She is aware of career stagnation, but she is taking steps toward renewal within a reasonable time.

Both of these situations illustrate the issues and barriers to change. Furthermore, they illustrate the challenge of not only committing to a change in career, but actually executing the change. In Jim's case some change is necessary, if for no other reason than his health. However, the barrier for him is resistance to serious consideration of alternatives. In his case, the resistance may go deeper than just a career issue. While a professional career counselor may help Jim sort out the job-related issues if he is willing to go that route, consideration of deeper emotional issues might best be resolved in a relationship with a mental health professional. Since Jim is also resistant to seeking counseling services, caring family members and/ or his cardiologist may be needed to push things in this direction.

As for Julia, since the transition can be gradual, the barrier associated with change is much less or non-existent. Fear of loss is no longer an issue. Thus, resistance may be replaced by enthusiasm in developing and executing strategies to make life better and more meaningful as time progresses.

So, what can we learn from this? How can we break through our own barriers to change when we really want to make a career or job change? Planning for gradual change, as in Julia's case, is one strategy. Once alternative careers are identified, planning can include training or education followed by part-time or volunteer experience. A gradual change of this nature might have eased the way for Don as well.

Continuously identifying and staying in the path of job opportunities is another strategy for breaking through barriers to change. Excellent job opportunities, however they present themselves, can quickly erase resistance to immediate change or speed the process of gradual career change. Even if you are not actively looking, you can be proactive by developing and maintaining an active network of colleagues with whom you discuss jobs and job opportunities; by keeping your social networking profiles, such as LinkedIn, up to date; and by periodically updating your resume.

In Jim's case, change of self-paradigm was a huge issue as it is for many people whose identity is inseparable from their profession. Chapter 5 addresses additional strategies for gradual change that target change of self-paradigm.

Finally, when resistance to change is dysfunctional, not readily resolvable, or goes beyond the realm of self-help, then consultation with a career counselor or mental health professional may be the best path to achieving fulfillment in career and other life areas. If you are hesitant about taking this step, the information in Chapters 29, 30, and 31 may be helpful.

CHAPTER 5[3]

Escaping the Paradigm of Ourselves[4]

Maria's Secret Desire

Maria is a high-volume real estate sales agent in Southern California. She has done this for 15 years and does quite well financially. She is well-known and sought after by new clients because of her sales record and her ability to relate so well to people from all walks of life. She loves helping people, but she is worn out by the pressure of sales and always trying to please everyone. Her colleagues see her as extremely competent and envy her sales acumen, so she never divulges her growing dissatisfaction with her career. Due to the stress she experiences,

Photo by Johnhain

---

3 Fernando Narvaez, Esq. was the primary author of a blog article on this topic, based on his experiences in working with Social Security disability claimants. This chapter reflects both his experiences, and experiences of the author of this book combined with research on change in self-concept.

4 Throughout the book the terms "self-paradigm" and "paradigm of ourselves" are used interchangeably.

she takes medication for her nerves and sees a mental health counselor weekly.

Maria's secret desire is to become a social worker and work in a youth development program within the Latino community where she grew up. Now that she is set financially and can be a role model, she wants to give back her time and effort to troubled teens from dysfunctional families who are headed in the wrong direction.

She knows achieving this goal will be a long road, with the education and training needed, but she thinks she can do it. Although she believes she has the personal desire and commitment, will she really be able to make such a major career change and see herself as something other than a real estate agent?

The journey of making a change to a different career or a substantially different job comes with various challenges. Many of these are obvious or clearly identifiable as in Maria's case, such as "do I need further education or licensing, etc.?" However, some may be completely hidden from our path and therefore, we are unaware that they even exist. In other words, we cannot acknowledge what we don't know.

> **To overcome the paradigm of ourselves, we need to be able to visualize ourselves as being someone else and doing something different. We need to be able to shift the way we view ourselves.**

Who Am I . . . What Am I?

Of the hidden challenges in making a major career change, none can be more elusive than the paradigm of ourselves. By the time we reach mid-career in a single occupation or a few related jobs, we have grown to see ourselves from one perspective: "This is what I've *always* done." "This is what I went to school for." "I've never done anything else in my life!" "This is how people know and respect me."

These are the things we tell ourselves when we're trapped in the paradigm of ourselves. We simply cannot envision ourselves as something different. As we saw with Jim, the physician in chapter 4, what we *do* has become who we *are*. This is what we call the "paradigm of ourselves."

When we are faced with the notion of changing our careers, it's not always enough to "see" what else is out there; or even to try to seek a new career or job based on such factors as skills, interests, and a work environment where we might fit. If we can't move beyond the paradigm of ourselves, we can't move from a mental commitment to making a change, to actually executing the change.

To overcome the paradigm of ourselves, we need to be able to visualize ourselves as being someone else and doing something different. We need to be able to shift the way we view ourselves. The challenge becomes greater as the transition we wish to make becomes farther removed from what we were doing before.

In Maria's case, a career change from real estate broker to social worker requires a major paradigm shift because of the huge differences in the occupations and industries. Had she wanted to change from a real estate agent to real estate broker that would only involve a minor shift that fits within the expected career path of a real estate agent. Neither she, nor any of her family, friends, or colleagues would even blink an eye about that change.

Similarly, with Jim, if he were to make a change in medical specialty or become a medical director of a clinic, no significant shift in self-paradigm would be needed. He would still be a physician. However, if he chose to become an engineer, the shift would need to be larger. Becoming a commercial artist would require even a greater self-paradigm shift.

With the benefit of the information era, there is an abundance of resources that can bring ideas as to what else we can do given our experience and skills. But for those trapped in a "self-paradigm," being told what other careers exist or even going through a process of career assessment and exploration is not necessarily enough to shift the paradigm to incorporate who we would be in the new occupation.

Why does this happen? Because most of us who have invested years of education or on-the-job training, plus years and years of practice, have solidified our concept of who we are, as have others. We have come to the point that we simply cannot envision ourselves as doing something else and therefore *being* someone else. Not only have we invested our time, money, and effort, but there is a natural fear of the unknown when presented with the notion of possibly starting over. Will the new identity afford me the same or better self-esteem, and respect from others? Will others see me as a different person than I want to be?

This can be seen in career professionals such as attorneys, accountants, teachers, or physicians. Other examples can be seen in skilled or semi-skilled careers, such as truck drivers, who may not be able to see themselves doing something while sitting at a desk or in a job that does not involve driving. We have heard . . . "but I've been driving a truck all my life, I don't know how to do anything else." However, it's not just "I don't know how to do anything else"; it's also "I can't see myself as doing anything else, nor can anyone I know."

Breaking Out

How does someone break free of the paradigm of ourselves trap? Research suggests that how other people view you strongly influences how you ultimately view yourself. This can be seen in Maria's case, since she was viewed as no less than a "master" real estate agent. Moving out of this role would destroy the image others have of her, and thus influence the image she has of herself.

Maria addressed this issue with her mental health counselor, who was also experienced in career counseling. Understanding the need for her to change her self-paradigm, the counselor suggested that Maria begin to engage part-time in social tasks that expose her to the social work occupation. This would accomplish two purposes. First, she will find out directly what a social worker does on a day-to-day basis, and to some extent experience it. Second, she will do it in the presence of others who will observe her engagement, give her feedback, and simultaneously see her in this role. This will give her the beginnings of what it will feel like to be, as well as be perceived as, a social worker.

Some specific tasks would involve doing informational interviews followed by "shadowing." Informational interviews are discussions with those in the field to find out more about what they do, their challenges and opportunities, as well as positives and negatives of the occupation. Shadowing would let Maria follow one or more social workers and, maybe, assist with some tasks for a few days at a time. The counselor suggested that these experiences be arranged through Maria's personal contacts in the Latino community where she wanted to eventually work and through social media connections on LinkedIn and Facebook.

For longer-term experiences, volunteer (unpaid) work can be arranged in some settings, or paid internships can be explored. Although these were not feasible for Maria, because of her real estate work commitments, such alternatives can further help in rapid transitioning to a new self-paradigm. This can also reveal if the new career you're considering isn't a good fit after all. Either one can be a good outcome.

So, if you're seeking a substantially different career path and changing your self-paradigm is an important barrier, once you begin to see yourself as what you want to be, and others begin to perceive you the same way, it becomes easier to bridge the gap from thought to action. Changing your self-paradigm can provide stronger drive, focus, and courage to take the necessary steps to make the change.

CHAPTER 6

How Much of a Change is Really Needed?

Photo by John Gillenwater

Must It Be a Huge Change?

Does every career change need to be huge and disruptive of life as you know it? Julia, the attorney, and Andrea, the teacher, kept their changes small and gradual. Larry, the government executive, engineered a small change in the same job. They all achieved the goals of avoiding or managing stagnation.

When job dissatisfaction builds after years of working in a job or career, it's not unusual to want to consider a *major* change. After all, feeling unfulfilled, devoid of passion, or simply "burned out" in your work takes its toll. When this happens, you may get to a point of no longer being able to tolerate the situation, feeling "I've got to do something." Often that something generates thoughts about nothing less than a major change in career. However, that could be an overreaction to the exasperation you feel.

I sometimes get calls from potential clients who feel an urgent need to make a change from their long-time career. The call is sometimes a desperation move based on a particularly traumatic day during a tough period at work. It's not an indicator that a total life upheaval is the answer, but that's how it feels.

Considering what's known as the Pareto Principle or 80/20 rule, even minor changes can make a substantial difference.

When you really think through embarking on a major change, actually doing it, or even making the commitment to do it, can quickly become unrealistic. The toll may be too great, with additional uncertainties about the future, re-education and training, reduction in salary, and reduced or higher medical benefits costs. You may conclude that it's just not worth it. Will a new career be any better than what you have now? If these thoughts have been going through your mind, you're not unusual. You're thinking clearly!

The good news is that you can develop and carry out a renewal strategy to restore work passion and meaning in your life, even if you don't make a major career change.

Limiting Change to What's Needed

So, what alternatives exist for limiting change without a major life upheaval?

Let's look at this from the perspective of what we call "the intersection principle" as described in detail in chapter 7. The idea is to create or restore a work situation in which your strongest skills, interests, and best-fit environment intersect or are congruent with your job. So, let's start by looking at those factors currently contributing most to your unhappiness, and then select an approach to incremental change with the lowest potential for upending the rest of your life.

1. **Your skills.** Do you have the skills to do your job at a high proficiency level? Do you get to use your best skills vs. mostly your mediocre or poorer skills? If you get to use your best skills, do you enjoy using them?

2. **Your interests.** Have you had periods of sustained interest in your field of work, not just your current job? For example, if you are a mechanical engineer, do you really like the work in that discipline?

3. **Your work environment.** This is often a critical factor contributing to dissatisfaction. Are you having difficulty meeting your employer's performance expectations? Does your workload leave time for little else in your life? Is the stress of strained relationships with peers or supervisors overriding satisfaction you would otherwise get from your work? What other factors in your work environment block enjoyment of your work?

Restoring a More Optimal Intersection with Limited Change

If by using the intersection principle, you can identify the core issues that interfere most with passion and meaning in your work, you can make some changes. Considering what's known as the Pareto Principle or 80/20 rule, even minor changes can make a substantial difference.

The 80/20 rule states that roughly 80% of effects come from 20% of the causes. So first, state and rank the top causes of your unhappiness related to your skills, interests, and work environment. Then determine what limited changes can be made. For example, using a composite from clients with whom I've worked, top causes and potential changes might look something like this:

1. **Environment:** "I can't keep up with the work. My supervisor keeps saying I need to do more and I am already working 60

hours a week. She doesn't understand. It's too much. I feel burned out and am afraid of losing my job."

2. **Skills:** "I like being an engineer and have some good successes over my 25-year career. However, the project I've been working on for the past 2 years stretches my knowledge compared to others on my work team. I can't keep up with them because I'm not using my strongest engineering skills."

Since interests are not one of the top causes of unhappiness in this example, the 80/20 rule would not require including it in considering change.

So, what are some limited readjustments that can be made? In this example, skills don't entirely match the work volume requirements. So, one option is to improve skills. That could involve working with the supervisor to develop a training plan and opportunities to carry it out. This would be of benefit to everyone, since work quality of the team would potentially improve, and it would also reduce the pressure to work 60 hours a week to keep up with co-workers. An environmental option is to request transfer to another project or to develop relationships inside the organization that would lead to another project that better fits your skillset.

Managing Work Interactions and Emotions

Environmental dissatisfactions can also be managed by taking actions to directly reduce emotional tension. A simple option is to air out issues with a supervisor. If an honest, trusting relationship exists or can be nurtured, setting up weekly or monthly meetings to vent or discuss work place challenges can ease tension and solve problems that otherwise feed resentments and work dissatisfaction. Working lunches or coffee breaks can provide other opportunities for this. I find that surprisingly few employees attempt to initiate this option without encouragement to try it.

Stress-reduction strategies, such as learning and practicing mindful meditation, progressive muscle relaxation, and coaching or counseling, can also help. The point is, even seemingly minor changes are almost always available, and can make a substantial difference in restoring passion and meaning in a job.

If you are experiencing chronic depression, anxiety, or other emotional dysfunction, this can increase environmental stress and ability to use skills. These can generate or worsen conflicts with co-workers and supervisors; affect ability to concentrate and persist on tasks; impact attendance; influence quality of decision making; and govern overall ability to retain jobs. This isn't an unusual reason for experiencing job stagnation. Again, the good news is that with recognition of the problems, limited actions can be taken to eliminate or mitigate the effects. Emotional dysfunction is covered in more detail in chapters 29 and 30.

Sammy the Sensitive—More Extensive, but Still Limited Changes

Sometimes, regardless of all efforts at resolving conflicts, incompatibility with a particular work setting is the root cause of stagnation. When this is the case, the next level of limited change would be to seek the same or similar type of job in another department of your current organization. A change of supervisor and scenery can often make a difference, particularly if simple attempts to reduce tension fail, and internal emotional dysfunction is not a major contributor.

Sammy was an administrative assistant in the shipping department of a large company. He was constantly in conflict with his boss. His supervisor was well thought of by most employees, but Sammy was particularly sensitive to how work criticisms were presented to him. He was highly competent at his work but would get very angry and defensive when asked to make minor changes to what he thought should be done.

Finally, Sammy's supervisor gave him a written admonishment regarding a need to change his behavior. Sammy got so mad that he went to the Human Resources Department and requested a transfer. Since he was known to be a highly competent organizer, but somewhat volatile, the manager of production operations, who needed someone to help him with an administrative reorganization, agreed to take Sammy.

Sammy flourished in this environment. The manager appreciated his ability to get tasks done independently and in a way that made operational support much more effective. Interestingly, Sammy also handled criticism better from this manager, probably a result of both a better fit in the setting, but also from what he learned from his dysfunctional behavior in the shipping department.

The point of this story is to illustrate how a change of environment can turn things around. However, I wouldn't recommend Sammy's confrontational method of requesting the change. He was lucky it worked!

Entering Major Change Territory

You can take change to the next level by seeking the same job in a different organization. This can address finding a better environmental fit without changing careers. But, this could mean committing to an extended job search, possible relocation, salary and benefit changes, and the uncertainties of a totally new organization and work environment. It's the beginning of what we have defined as major change, a career or life upending change.

The next increment would involve career change, but on a limited basis. For example, for the mechanical engineer who communicates well and has strong influencing skills, transferability to other related careers is possible. Seeking an industrial sales engineer or sales representative job might be alternatives. This change could involve using best skills and interests, as well as finding a best-fit environment. It's a more extensive major change.

The Ultimate Change

Finally, the most substantial change is a new career unrelated to the original one. This is magnified further if you were always an employee and also now plan to start your own business or a corporation. This, of course, is the riskiest and potentially most upending option, but one that can also create opportunity for a new, life-enriching start.

So, in looking at all the options for finding renewed passion or meaning in your work, even the minimal change approaches can have a high yield. On the other hand, if after considering the alternatives, you still think a totally new career might be your best chance for self-renewal, go for it! However, before making a major change of this nature, consider consulting with a career professional for assessment, confirmation, planning, and coaching. This will give you direction and assurance that you are making the right move, in the best way, and support as you move forward.

PART 3

Choosing a New Career or Job

As discussed in Part 2, making a change in your career or even your job in mid- or late career is often a major undertaking. A career is an occupation or profession, usually requiring special training or education, such as banker, electrician, teacher, auto mechanic, accountant, cook, attorney, writer, etc. It can consist of a single job or several related jobs. If you've been in a single, or even multiple careers, by the time you have worked 10–15 years you usually have a lot of invested time in education, training, and work experience. For this reason, making a career change is more significant than changing jobs. However, a change in job, particularly if it is in a new organization, industry, type of business, location, or crosses occupation or profession lines can be a major undertaking as well. In either case, due to the potential for significant life disruption, making good choices is important when using the strategy of career or job change for renewal.

The following chapters present information and tools for making choices in mid-career and later based on a framework we call the "intersection principle." Using this approach is particularly useful if you have developed skills in one or more fields.

Applying the intersection principle to choosing a new career or job builds on the fact that by mid-career, you don't usually need to start from square one in planning. Rather, you can now plan from a different perspective. You already have work experience, skills, history, and knowledge about your capabilities and interests, and some knowledge about the environments in which you do your best work. You also have maturity and wisdom that you may not have had when you made early career decisions. You can now renew and revitalize by building on *your past and creating new ways of achieving a sense of work passion and meaning.*

On the other hand, you may still have time to make a total change in direction if that turns out to be the best path. The intersection principle provides a basis for you to plan for that as well.

CHAPTER 7
New Jobs and Careers

Photo by Portal Dos Vistas

Chris's Dilemma

Chris, 41, has a degree in business administration and has had seven different administrative support and sales jobs in finance, medical services, and telecommunications organizations over the past 18 years. All his jobs were minimally challenging to his skills, and after a year or so, none seemed very interesting or of great importance. He moved from job to job based on whether he could make more money. Due to his quickly waning interest, he functioned in each job as only an average worker.

You are most likely to feel passion and meaningfulness in a job that occurs at the intersection of your best skills, your strongest interests, your best-fit environment, and the best matching job opportunities.

Chris was laid off eight months ago from a management analyst job during company downsizing. He held that job for three years and was finding it increasingly boring. He wasn't motivated or interested in doing more than the minimum required, so laying him off wasn't a great loss for the company. He's been looking for something since the layoff and has gotten only two first interviews with no job offers.

His search has been general, not focusing on any one type of job or industry. In the interim, he's been working as a barista part-time and doing some substitute teaching, which gives him a minimum income. At this point, he's desperate to find something full-time and thinks he would take anything that came along.

Anyone who has been searching a while for a skilled or professional job knows that it can be a difficult and humbling experience. For Chris, it's the first time it's taken him this long, and now the discouragement he's feeling is impacting his ability to keep at it. He's uncertain about his search strategy and is realistically concerned that his lack of direction as well as his history of not being a "stellar" worker is impacting. However, he is a serious job hunter and is making a legitimate effort to find a new job.

How could Chris approach his situation most constructively? While he is feeling desperate now, the work pattern that has been developing over 18 years has gotten him to this point. So, should he be looking at a new way of searching for a job? Should he be looking at a change in career? How can he approach this situation to reverse what could be considered a long-term stagnating pattern? How can he move into a different mode of viewing how he chooses the type of work he wants to do, the jobs he searches for, and how he actually looks for a job, with the goal of finding more fulfilling work?

The Intersection Principle

If you've been trying to follow "flavor of the day" job search techniques, applying for jobs can be confusing. Every blog writer has a different opinion, and the trend of opinions and advice changes every few months.

However, we find that certain basic precepts can serve well in positioning yourself not only to get a job, but to get the right job, one that elicits a passion for and a sense of meaning in what you do, as well as serving an employer's desire to get the best, most motivated employees in today's or tomorrow's job market; in other words, employees who work with a passion. These precepts include keeping the focus of your search on synchronizing your strongest interests and skills, most compatible work settings, and the jobs you target in your search.

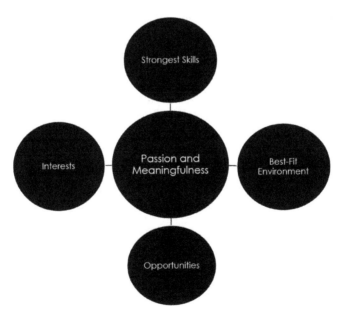

The intersection principle puts this all together as a way to guide you toward the goal of landing in the *right* job. It simply states that "you are most likely to feel passion and meaningfulness in a job that occurs at the intersection of your best skills, your strongest interests, your best-fit environment, and the best matching job opportunities."

It is a principle that deals with effectively putting career and job choices into practice in a way that maximally benefits you and an employer.

To illustrate some points, Bonnie Simon[5], who articulated the first pieces of the intersection principle, offers some real-life observations from her corporate experience regarding where skills and interests intersect with the best results:

"I noticed when working at a Fortune 100 corporation that there were people we called 'stars' who were really good at their jobs. They got a lot of attention from management, got promoted and made more money than the rest of us, but they also seemed to enjoy their jobs more. That's not surprising since they were very helpful to the organization and to the people they worked with. . . . Honestly, I think I was entering star territory with Information Technology Service Level Management."

Information Technology Service Level Management involved getting people in different technical departments to coordinate with each other. It entails a lot of data and negotiation. In Bonnie's case, her skills in analysis, building social relationships, and helping groups to solve problems made her good at putting intradepartmental agreements into place. She was able to do this despite lacking a full understanding of the technical workings of the software and hardware systems in question. What made her good at this job was that she was focused on using her strongest skills, not trying to compensate for her weaknesses in understanding details of the technology.

Job seekers often find themselves focused on trying to sell minimal skills they think employers will want. Then, when they get a

---

[5] Bonnie Simon, co-author of both this chapter and an earlier blog article on this topic, is a business owner, entrepreneur, and writer in Colorado Springs, CO. She worked in a professional capacity for Progressive Insurance for 10 years, and several non-profits prior to that. Bonnie has reviewed and written about the operations of over 150 small businesses in the Colorado Springs area in her blog at hungrychickenhomestead.com.

job, they try to compensate for whatever skills or experience they lack. This may not be the most constructive strategy.

Now Discover Your Strengths is a popular business book by Donald O. Clifton and Marcus Buckingham[6]. Bonnie heard of the book from a senior manager at her company. "The authors said it didn't make sense to spend one's life trying to become good at things one is weak on, and neglect improving the things one is strong in," Bonnie says. "That seems right to me. The 'stars' all got better at things they were really good at, and it made them great employees. So what if the star programmer has only moderate skill at writing? The key seemed to be finding where that strength was useful, not trying to be good at a weakness."

This doesn't imply that you can't improve on weaknesses, but the point is to capitalize on skills for which you are most likely to approach or achieve star-level strength.

Keep the Focus on What You Do Best AND What You Like Best

So, let's go back to Chris, the job seeker or maybe even career changer, and apply the intersection principle. Let's say he can identify not only all of his skills, but also his strongest skills. Then, of the strongest skills, which are the ones that have been of most interest in using?

Many skills, such as programming or facilitating work group coordination, can be used in a variety of career fields, such as medicine, banking, food service, or the arts. Since he has had experience in several fields, could he identify both the strong skills and fields that are of greatest interest to him?

Chris could even go one step further and do a more thorough analysis of his career interests. This could be done through testing and would help Chris clarify his general career interests and point to occupations most consistent with his overall interest pattern; that is, not only those things he likes, but also what he dislikes.

---

6   Buckingham, M. and Clifton, D. O. (2001). *Now discover your strengths*. New York; The Free Press

Discover the Right Work Environment

The next intersecting component is environment—the work context in which you use your skills and interests. Environment can include the industry, the types of people with whom you work or interact, the communication style within an organization, or other factors associated with where you work that could contribute to making you feel more passionate about what you do.

Would the "stars" to whom Bonnie refers have emerged in a small company with some already established stars, or different types of leaders or work styles, or in a different industry? If they didn't emerge as stars, would they have the level of passion for their work that, in combination with skills and interests, made them great employees?

Getting to the Intersection—Targeting and Finding the Right Job

After defining your best skills, the ones you are most interested in using, your general and occupational interests, and your best-fit environment, then comes perhaps the most critical component of the intersection principle: finding the opportunities. This starts the process of getting the right job directly or getting the most compatible job after you prepare for a new career. It's a point at which many job seekers lose their way.

Rather than simply looking for a job, the task now becomes one of skillfully targeting the job search toward the intersection point of skills, interests, and environments. This requires using the right job search methods to keep the ball rolling in the targeted direction.

All your energy is now focused on finding the opportunities, getting interviews, and then landing in a job that uses your best skills, is consistent with what you love to do or are passionate about on a day to day basis, in a place that you can thrive and in which your employer, customers, clients or patients believe you are, or can be, a "star."

A Change in Careers

Using the intersection principle as a guide, taking a thorough look at skills and interests in mid-career can sometimes lead to unexpected results. What starts out with the intent of finding a job may end up being the start of changing careers.

In Chris's case, he found that he was particularly skilled in public relations, such as dealing with the media and presenting himself on TV when he was infrequently called upon to substitute for someone. He felt good about himself when he did this because he thought it was important. It also required him to "think on his feet," which was exciting.

His interest inventory results also confirmed interests similar to people who do this work and are satisfied with it. He subsequently decided to go back to school for a master's degree in public relations and eventually found a job as a media relations specialist with a large medical equipment manufacturer. This time, when he did his job search, he targeted specific jobs he knew would use his best skills and interests. He also focused on employers in an industry in which he had prior experience and which he knew made products that significantly contributed to advances in healthcare. He could easily support that effort in media relations.

Finally, based on his research through prior contacts, he narrowed his search to companies that were consistent with his work style. When he applied for jobs using this approach, within two months he found a highly compatible job, and an employer eager to hire him.

A Win-Win Situation

The intersection principle applies as a basis to consider both career and job changes. And, when it comes to finding jobs, you might as well focus where you have the highest chance of experiencing passion for the work you do, feeling what you are doing is meaningful, AND ending up with an employer or customers (if you are self-employed) that can appreciate and benefit from your passion and skill.

Later chapters address components of the intersection principle and related topics in more detail. Job search strategies are addressed in Part 4—Landing the Right Job.

CHAPTER 8

Identifying Job Skills[7]

Photo by Geralt

Melissa's Lost Opportunity

Melissa, a 54-year-old recent widow, needed to return to work after three years of full-time caregiving. She was interviewing for an executive assistant job at a small waste disposal company. Melissa had a strong 20-year work background in sales and marketing, as well in several prior jobs as an administrative coordinator and project manager.

During the interview, her skills were discussed, which she also listed on her resume. Since this company was interested in expanding

---

7   Concepts in this chapter are based in part upon analyzing skills and transferable skills of at least 4000-5000 persons in the past 17 years, as of the date of this writing.

business, she talked about her achievements in selling new products and her proficiency in market research techniques. However, she forgot that in one of her administrative jobs she helped write a proposal for a federal contract. She used skills learned in researching government procurement regulations and in composing effective proposal language. Her employer was awarded the contract. She also didn't think to mention or even remember that with another small employer, she learned enough technical IT skills to help the company avoid paying for outside assistance with software installations or computer maintenance.

If Melissa had done her research, asked the right questions during the interview, and been in touch with all her skills, she could have shown herself to be a strong asset for this business. For example, they could easily increase their scope of business through government contracting and she could help get them there.

Further, as a small company, an executive assistant who knows computers could have saved them thousands of dollars yearly in outside computer maintenance costs. The interviewer liked Melissa, but she did not demonstrate as much value as other candidates because her "hidden skills" remained hidden. Thus, she did not get the job.

So, as you can see with Melissa, if you are in mid-career or later, the skills segment of applying the intersection principle is critical. By this time, the skills you've developed and how well you can use them demonstrate your ability to learn and apply the proficiencies needed to do a job well. Unless you will be changing careers or developing more complex skills, in most cases, it isn't necessary to assess your intelligence or academic aptitude like with someone first selecting a career. Your skills already tell what you can learn and do. On the other hand, if you wish to make a change that requires new and different skill sets, particularly requiring more advanced education and training, chapter 10 addresses factors that need further consideration.

What are Skills?

So, what job skills do you have? Sit down and see if you can write a list. If you're like most people, you may come up with four or five broad categories of things you know how to do or do in your current job, such as planning, information technology, customer service, or helping people. Or you may list that you're good with numbers or that you have artistic talent. You may even list the most important tasks you do in your job or profession.

When we ask people about their skills, review resumes, and look at articles on resume writing, the meaning of skills is not uniform, and often overlaps with tasks, talents, and aptitudes. Thus, to do this exercise effectively, the first thing we need to do is clarify what we mean and don't mean by skills.

Skills are the learned, specific *proficiencies* and *knowledge* needed to do a job. They are the mental work tools you bring to the table that demonstrate your value in completing important elements of your job.

Skills are NOT the tasks you do, such as treating patients or litigating cases. Skills ARE the *underlying* proficiencies and knowledge necessary to accomplish the tasks in a competent manner. If you are a physician, in order to treat patients, you must have proficiency in medical diagnostics, prescribing medications, and knowledge of disease processes. As an attorney, to litigate cases, you must have proficiency in taking depositions, communicating complex legal information, and knowledge of applicable law. Specificity is important because if you are too general in describing skills, e.g., communicating, there is nothing unique about what you know or can do; most people can communicate to some extent.

Skills are also NOT the inborn talents you have, or your aptitudes. You may apply your talent or aptitudes to developing a skill such as musical talent to playing the piano, or numerical aptitude to financial auditing. Talents and aptitudes may be important in the long run, but they are not the skills you possess now.

Hidden and Transferable Skills

In addition to your current skills, there are usually a lot more skills from your past that you haven't thought about or have forgotten about. These are your "hidden" skills. Few of us are in touch with all the skills we actually have, because they are not in our everyday focus.

So, many skills are out-of-sight, out-of-mind, hidden or forgotten and therefore not much use to you or anyone else. For Melissa, not remembering her proposal writing and computer maintenance skills probably cost her the job. Skills can also be transferable. That is, as with Melissa, her proposal-writing skills could easily be transferred to another job.

Create Your Skills Inventory

Now that we have defined the meaning of skills, try doing an inventory of your skills using the *Skills Inventory Worksheets* in Appendix A of this book. The skills can include not only those that have a clear relationship to your current job or career, but also those that are not seemingly work related.

Non-work skills can become useful in some work contexts or projects, or when considering new jobs or changes in career. Only include skills that you can still use today, with or without a little brush-up if necessary:

- Skills learned through jobs—in past and current employment, as well as in special assignments and projects.
- Skills learned through education or training—include college, technical schools, workshops, and in-house training courses.
- Skills learned through hobbies, volunteer work, home projects, community work, leadership activities and so forth.

As you go through this exercise, you will become progressively aware of unrealized or forgotten skills. Think this through and expand the list as far as you can. Avoid leaving out skills that might seem trivial, such as typing or using different types of office software or organizing children's recreational events. Even if you are in a specialized professional field, some incidental skills can turn out to differentiate your value from others. Maybe you're a skilled bridge player, golfer, or chess player. While you won't put these skills on your resume, reviewing them on a list of all skills before a job interview could put you in a position to remember abilities or knowledge that could help make a connection during the interview.

Writing a list of skills can be difficult. When I've worked with clients on this, regardless of their background, the task of how to write a skill effectively usually takes several iterations. To do this correctly the first time, follow these instructions carefully:

1. Re-read the meaning of skills in this chapter. Precisely understanding what skills are and how to express them is the point at which doing this exercise independently typically breaks down.

2. As you begin to think about your skills, using Part I of the worksheet, conceptualize and write each one in *one* of the following formats:

    a. Start with the "ing" form of a verb, such as "preparing," "operating,", or "teaching." Examples are:

- Preparing federal tax returns
- Operating power sawing machines
- Teaching conversational Spanish

Using the "ing" verb has the advantage of communicating active and present proficiency in doing something.

    b. Starting with "knowledge of." Examples are:

- Knowledge of Microsoft office software
- Knowledge of federal contracting rules
- Knowledge of procurement principles

Knowledge statements communicate competency in subject matter implying proficiency in tasks that require such knowledge.

    c. A concise statement such as:

- Public speaking
- Consultative selling
- Public relations
- Procurement
- Program evaluation
- Grant writing

The main criteria is assuring that the statement as written is truly a *proficiency* that underlies accomplishing important job elements, and not simply a description of a task.

3. Proficiencies or knowledge can often be expressed at various levels of specificity and complexity. You will need to find the most descriptive level for what you are trying to communicate. Consider the following:

    a. Level A: Teaching
    b. Level B: Teaching Spanish
    c. Level C: Teaching basic conversational Spanish

Level A is very general and implies that you can do any type of teaching. Level B suggests your teaching skills are limited to Spanish, but also implies that you have enough knowledge of the Spanish language to teach it. Level C is more specific, but more limited because it implies only a knowledge of basic Spanish.

4. In preparing your initial inventory, it's best if you list separate skills and then combine later. You might have originally listed:

   a. Teaching
   b. Speaking and writing fluent Spanish
   c. Knowledge of multiple Spanish dialects

   Your final skill statement probably would have been "Teaching Spanish" because although your experience was mainly in teaching conversational Spanish, your skills were good enough to teach Spanish at any level. Level A would have been too broad if you wanted to emphasize the special subject matter expertise in Spanish. Level C would have been too narrow because it implies limited knowledge of Spanish.

5. Even though you will eventually combine skills, the deeper you drill down in levels on your initial list of skills, the more proficiencies and knowledge you will find you have. It's not unusual for a full list for someone in mid-career or later, drilled down and uncombined, to have 30–50 skills.

6. After completing your list in Part 1 of the worksheet, using Part 2, combine and consolidate to a list of no more than 10–15 skills.

7. Using instructions in Part 3 of the worksheet, rate skills on the combined list *based on how well you do at them.*

8. Using Part 4 if the worksheet, list skills on the combined list that you rated 4 and 5. These are your strongest skills.

Keep both the uncombined and combined lists available. They will serve you well when writing a resume, when identifying and applying for jobs to which your skills match or can transfer, and when selling yourself in job interviews. They can also be used with your current employer when demonstrating what you are capable of doing in your current job, and in making others aware of your previously unknown skills when promotion opportunities arise.

You may find that having a good handle on all your skills can also help in building your confidence and self-esteem. Once the full inventory of skills is documented, most people are surprised and pleased at what they actually can do!

Transferring Your Skills

If you are looking to switch careers, transferable skills analysis can be helpful in identifying different jobs that use the same skills you have and which would require limited or no additional training to perform. You can try to figure that out yourself, using your skills inventory and resources described in chapter 11. Or you could use the results of the skills inventory in combination with a simple transferable skills online tool (http://www.myskillsmyfuture.org/) and the accompanying career exploration resources.

If that doesn't work, there are computer resources and software that can help with the assistance of a career counselor or a rehabilitation counselor experienced in transferable skills analysis technology. Rehabilitation counselors often use this when assisting people with disabilities to find new careers consistent with remaining capacities. However, you do not need to have a disability to benefit from their assistance with transferable skills analysis.

You can find directories of career counselors through the National Career Development Association (https://tinyurl.com /yagp49j8) and certified rehabilitation counselors through the International Association of Rehabilitation Professionals (https:// tinyurl.com/ybvp4wjy) or the Commission on Rehabilitation Counselor Certification (https://tinyurl.com/yc6gtphz).

CHAPTER 9
Assessing Your Job Interests[8]

Photo by ID 97318901 © Halifah Rahmansyah | Dreamstime.com

An Unhappy Engineer

Karen is a 40-year-old electrical engineer. She's worked for the same small engineering firm since finishing her college degree. She studied engineering because her parents said it was a good field for a woman. They believed the opportunities would be greater because there were not many women engineers.

Since Karen was good in math and tended to follow the advice of her parents, she enrolled in an engineering program at college. She

---

8 The author has had no business associations with any of the publishers or sponsors of materials cited in this chapter, other than to purchase and/or use testing materials for professional purposes.

got through a state school BSEE program with a B average and went directly to work. From the beginning, she did not particularly like the work and she wasn't among the better engineers, but she had a good job with a better salary than most of her friends working in other fields. So, she just plugged away during the week and looked forward to her weekends. Her interests were clearly not consistent with her work, and she felt that she was not achieving much with her career.

Now, after 17 years in the field, Karen is feeling she needs to do something more stimulating and meaningful. She is annoyed and resentful that she was not the one who made the decision to become an engineer. She didn't carefully look at her interests, or fields in which she might find the most satisfaction. She blindly followed her parents' advice. She is now divorced, has no children, and an unsatisfying career has become the most significant part of her life.

> **If you're looking for passion and meaning in your work, it's crucial to be interested in what you do.**

It's not unusual to enter a first career for the wrong reasons. In fact, many teens and young adults choose occupations and jobs based on what friends or family tell them, what they see on TV and on social media, or fields where the job market is growing or salaries are highest. This is fine if the occupations are consistent with abilities and basic interest patterns. Ability and aptitude show up early in training. If one doesn't have what's needed, they probably won't be successful completing education or training, or performing satisfactorily once working.

Interests are another story. As Karen's history demonstrates, you can enter an occupation and work for many years with mediocre interests. However, as Karen now realizes in mid-career, if you're looking for passion and meaning in your work, it's crucial to be interested in what you do. In fact, if you have little or no interest, you might have difficulty getting up every morning to face doing it.

On the other hand, if you have intense interest, you'll look forward to going to work every day. For many of us, interests take on more significance in mid-career with the realization that the career timeline is shortening . . . there's not that much time left, . . . and that work can be a major medium for finding life meaning and making important life contributions.

Interests—Part of the Puzzle

So, if you're thinking about a change, how can you choose a direction that will sustain your interest and passion for work over the long term?

Figuring out your career interests can be tricky. You may be able to identify things you like to do and some that you don't. But, it's not likely that you will remember all the things you're interested in and be able to relate them to corresponding jobs. Also, you're probably not aware of the full range of career and job options consistent with your interests.

Without this information, it's difficult to consider all the alternatives and make an informed decision on the job or career content that would generate a new and continuing sense of passion for what you do. You probably have also thought about some jobs that would seem really interesting, more interesting than what you do now. But how would you feel about them once you started doing them. After all, you don't want to invest in starting a new direction only to find out after a few years that you're back in the same place.

To maximize satisfaction in your work over the long term, your interests should also synchronize favorably with your skills and best-fit environment, as described in the intersection principle in chapter 7. The best skills you use should correspond with your interests, and your interests should be a consideration in determining your best-fit work environment.

If you're looking for a new job, following that path then allows you to target job opportunities that will bring you the greatest passion for what you do and where you do it, as well as resulting enthusiasm and satisfaction from who you do it for—your employer, customers, clients, or patients.

Exploring Five Dimensions of Interests

To do all of this, we can explore our interests from five perspectives:

1. Determine the activities we enjoy that can relate to a job, such as fixing mechanical things, writing stories, or selling products.
2. Look at how closely our personality "types" based on interests compare to the "types" of those who populate various occupations. In this way, we would be looking for environments of people similar to ourselves.
3. Compare our total interest pattern, likes and dislikes, with those who enter various occupations and maintain satisfaction in what they do years later. This is a good predictive measure of how we might maintain satisfaction over time with a job or career.
4. Relate interests to the best skills we have. That is, of the job skills at which we are best, which are we most interested in using?
5. Target places to search for a job. What industry is of most interest to us?

Of course there are other factors to consider, such as salary and the realities of pursuing and finding stable work in the right location. The intersection principle forces focus first on expanding the possibilities for finding maximum passion for and meaning in what you do and where you do it, and then narrowing decisions later, as necessary.

Self-Assessing Interests Per the Intersection Principle

Here is a procedure consistent with the intersection principle that you can use to assess most aspects of your own interests. It incorporates steps 1, 2, 4, and 5 above. Step 3 requires a more sophisticated tool covered in the next section.

1. For self-assessment of career and job options, John Holland's personality theory provides a solid basis for exploration[9]. Career interests are organized as one or a combination of six

---

9   The Development, Evolution, and Status of Holland's Theory of Vocational Personalities: Reflections and Future Directions for Counseling Psychology." *Journal of Counseling Psychology,* Vol 57(1), 2010, 11-22.

personality types. Single and combined types correspond to the working environments of groups of related occupations, based on similar types of people who gravitate to them. The Self Directed Search (SDS), originally developed by Holland, is the best tool for this self-assessment. You can complete this inventory, at low cost, online and get a detailed interpretive report at https://tinyurl.com/y8b4qmg4. The report includes links to occupations and related career information associated with your interests.

A free version of a similar inventory, is available at My Next Move (https://tinyurl.com/7x45pbm). However, the paid version gives the most comprehensive interpretive information per Holland's theory. Both assessments provide convenient links to the U.S. Department of Labor's O*NET (https://www.onetonline.org/) database of occupational information and other helpful resources for purposes of career and job exploration, based on inventory results.

2. Do a review of your interests with respect to your strongest skills. That is, of your strong skills, which ones do you enjoy using most? Factor out your mediocre or weaker skills. If you are developing skills you anticipate will become strong, include those. For example, if you have strong skills in creating software programs, in product marketing, and will soon have strong skills in using accounting software, which of these skills do you get the most enjoyment out of using? You can do this assessment without any further tools as long as you have done a good skills assessment that includes your hidden skills.

Appendix A provides instructions and forms for doing the hidden skills analysis on your own. If you used those forms, go to Part 4—List of Strongest Skills. For each of the skills listed, pencil in one of the following ratings for each skill:

1. I have no interest whatsoever in doing work using this skill.
2. I usually have very little interest in doing work involving this skill.
3. I feel neutral about doing work using this skill.
4. I am usually very interested in doing work involving this skill.
5. I intensely enjoy using this skill.

The skills you rated 4 or 5 are your strongest skills in which you have the most interest using.

3. Consider the industries in which you would prefer to work. Working in an industry environment for which you have an affinity should enhance the meaning and value you feel for what you do. For instance, using the example above, if you wanted to use your best skills in product sales, you have knowledge of software development, your career interests are consistent with sales and marketing jobs, AND you have a special affinity for the entertainment industry, you could potentially target your job search toward corporate sales work in electronic gaming software. Skills and interests in occupations can often transfer across industries, so there may be several targeting possibilities by industry. You can find an easy to use classification of industries and related occupations at O*NET (https://tinyurl.com /yc49nc4r). A more expansive list of industries can be found at OSHA's website (https://tinyurl.com/62fk2).

Beyond Self-Assessment of Interests

There are some tools that provide more comprehensive and sophisticated measures of career interests. For example, some interest inventories provide scales based on Holland's theory; scales that categorize basic interests, such as office management, culinary arts, marketing and advertising; plus scales that compare your likes and dislikes with people who are working in occupations in which they are satisfied.[10]

These tests also provide options for full computer interpretive profiles with resources that can help you explore options and make career decisions. Such inventories would be available through a career counselor who would also usually help with interpretation. You can find such services through college career centers, or privately through a career counselor listed in a reputable source such as the National Career Development Association Directory (https:// tinyurl.com/yd5qwelc).

So, had Karen, our unhappy engineer, carefully explored her interests with respect to her strong math skills, taken a broader range of

---

10   These examples are from the Strong Interest Inventory (Strong Interest Inventory. (2012). Sunnyvale: CPP.) one of several such inventories available for this purpose.

courses in college, and maybe taken an interest inventory, she might have considered other more suitable occupations. Examples might be mathematics teacher, statistician, financial analyst, financial planner, and accountant. Now, in mid-career and feeling unfulfilled in her work, the timing is right to regroup and consider careers and jobs in which she will have a sustained interest as a path to gaining a sense of passion and meaning for her future work.

CHAPTER 10

Capacity for Upgrading Education and Training

Tara's and John's Career Change Plans—Are They Achievable?

Tara is a 41-year-old legal secretary, married with two teen-agers, who is considering going back to school to eventually get a law degree. She has an associate degree from a community college in paralegal studies and 10 years of experience working for a small legal firm. Based on her experience, she believes she could do the work of a lawyer, an obvious major upgrade from her current job.

John, 38, works as an internal help desk specialist giving advice on solving hardware and software problems to employees of a large company. He has a year and a half of college and 15 years of on-job training, short courses, and experience in installing and trouble-shooting business software applications and technology equipment. John would like more challenging work, and opportunities to make more money. He would have a good chance to advance within his company if he had a bachelor's degree with skills in programming and systems analysis.

For some mid- or late career changers, new jobs and careers can be found using existing skills, or with minor upgrades. However, as in Tara's and John's cases, major changes are planned that will require a new, more complex set of skills. In those instances, other factors must be considered, namely having the general ability, and sometimes special aptitudes and talent to acquire the skills. They'll also need the right personal circumstances to complete education and training.

Abilities, Aptitudes, Talent, and Extraneous Factors

General ability or intelligence refers to a combination of personal characteristics that allow us to learn, understand, reason, and apply concepts and knowledge. Increasing levels of general ability are associated with being able to achieve higher levels of education, socioeconomic, and career status.

Aptitudes can be viewed as specialized abilities, or potential to develop skills in more specific areas. For example, use of language, numbers, and spatial reasoning are key factors that contribute to general ability. When measured by tests, these factors can be combined into a composite score indicating general ability or intelligence.

These three factors (language, numbers, and spatial reasoning) can also differ substantially from one another and be viewed as individual aptitudes. If you have above-average general ability, but are much stronger in numerical than language ability, you will probably find it easier to develop skills in engineering than in journalism. However, with high general ability and slightly above-average language aptitude, you could still develop skills as a journalist. It just might take more motivation and persistence.

Special aptitudes, such as in music or art, can be less related to general ability, but having them makes it easier to learn skills in these areas. Combined with unusual talent or innate skill, it might be easy to develop the highest levels of competence and achievement. For example, we might argue that the best musicians have an exceptional talent for playing music, as well as strong aptitude for learning and understanding advanced music theory.

So, if you're looking to make a major upgrade in skills, an assessment of your potential to do this is needed. Not only will factors such as general ability, aptitude, and talent need consideration; your motivation to learn, persistence, financial means, and family responsibilities and dynamics need to be factored in. Such extraneous factors have an influence, more so when ability and aptitude levels are at the lower end of what is usually required.

In Tara's case, she has experience with legal matters, how attorneys become qualified, and what they do. However, to get into law school, she would need to complete her bachelor's degree with good grades and achieve an acceptable score on the Law School Admissions Test (LSAT). Then she would need to get accepted into a local law school. If accepted, she would compete against other law students in a rigorous curriculum. Due to her circumstances, Tara would also need to work part-time to cover the costs and still contribute to family income.

What Are the Chances For Success?

Tara made mainly B and C grades in high school and college, even though she studied hard. Her SAT scores were average for those at her community college, but a little lower than average for students at the local state college that she plans to attend for a bachelor's degree. She took a practice LSAT exam and found that she did not score high enough at this point to have much chance of acceptance at a law school. However, she thinks that would change after getting a bachelor's degree.

The reality here is that even finishing a bachelor's degree is iffy, considering her overall life responsibilities. Then, assuming she did get accepted, getting through a rigorous law school program would be even more taxing. She would need to have exceptional persistence and stamina. Her plan would be very high risk for completion, even at a lower tier law school.

For John, the situation is different. He is single and has saved some money. In high school, he did best in math, earning mostly A's. Similarly, in college, the courses in which he got the highest grades were information technology and advanced algebra, all A's. He dropped out when he took a great job offer which gave him a chance to break into working with computer systems.

Before college he scored well above average on the SAT math section. He will have no problem getting accepted into a bachelor's program in information technology at the university he previously attended. He is now quite motivated to complete college and will have his employer's support to work half-time while he attends school. For John, the chances of developing the skills for successful major career change are high.

> **Before embarking on a major, potentially costly change, it's a good idea to do the best objective assessment that you can regarding your capabilities and the factors that might enhance or interfere with using them.**

The cases of Tara and John illustrate that prerequisite general ability and aptitudes are necessary to learn new skills. The more ability and aptitude one has for learning the skills in question, the easier it is to acquire them. This doesn't preclude learning the skills when ability and aptitudes are lower, but it's more difficult and may require more time and resources. These things are not insurmountable, but in Tara's case, she would need to have exceptional fortitude, as well as support from her family and employer, and probably from her school, to succeed.

Assessing Your Capacity to Develop a New and Different
Skill Set

How can general ability, aptitudes, talent, and mitigating factors be assessed? In John's case, based on his work successes, educational history, and testing, he could determine on his own that he has a high chance of success. Tara, on the other hand, would benefit from assistance of a career counselor to help her assess the reality of her goal, what she would need to do to get there, and alternative goals.

The point is, if you are considering a change in careers which requires an entirely new and different skill set, don't forget to consider your general ability, aptitudes, and talents. This is not an attempt to discourage anyone from pursuing a dream or from trying. Sometimes it's even necessary to try and fail in order to avoid feeling that you've let yourself down. However, the adage "you can do anything you really want to do" is a myth.

So, before embarking on a major, potentially costly change, it's a good idea to do the best objective assessment that you can regarding your capabilities and the factors that might enhance or interfere with using them. Consult a career counselor if necessary. Regardless of how interested or excited you are about starting a new, more advanced career journey, it will be to your long-term advantage to do a reality check on what you want to do.

CHAPTER 11

How to Find Information about Careers and Jobs

Photo by ID 97318901 © Halifah Rahmansyah | Dreamstime.com

If you are considering a new career or a change in careers or jobs, you may be struggling with how to find the right information to make a decision. It's a common issue I see in career counseling. Getting a reliable, unbiased picture of what a career field is really like can be difficult, particularly with emerging occupations and job specialties popping up all the time.

Focus Your Search

What are the best ways of finding what you need to know? The first step is to have some focus. You should have one or a few general fields in mind, or one or more specific jobs. For example, you may wish to explore jobs in the entire medical field, or maybe you want to look only at jobs in nursing, or perhaps just the job of a patient-care technician.

Unless you have some known jobs in mind, exploring occupations and jobs often starts with the more general fields. That will usually lead to looking deeper into more specific jobs of interest.

This doesn't mean that the process will always take a smooth, linear path. You may go from one general field to another and back again. Or you may start with a general field and some specific jobs to look at and end up circling back to other fields and jobs. However, usually you will eventually settle on one or a few specific choices.

Jack, one of my mid-career clients, knew he wanted a change, but could not settle on anything specific. In fact, one of his problems was that after 20 years of working, he was bouncing around from one field to another, and back again. We started with a focus on four diverse areas: human resources, customer service, business trainer, and business analyst.

To find enough information for decision-making, some of these fields required considerable drill-down into specific jobs. Human resources, which has numerous specialty areas as well as a generalist option, is an example. Others, such as business trainer, required only deeper exploration of the types of job openings, what different types of trainers do in different organizations, and their salaries.

Coolest Sources for an Information Search

Once you have a focus for your job search, you can choose the right resources to find out more. For general and moderately specific job searches such as Jack's, two of the most comprehensive sources are the U.S. Department of Labor's Occupational Outlook Handbook (OOH) (https://tinyurl.com/yd5qwelc) and the Occupational Information Network, called O*NET (https://www.onetonline .org/). Both are free and easily searchable online.

The OOH is published every other year and includes detailed information on 576 occupations, which covers about 83% of the jobs in the economy. For each occupation, it includes information about the nature of work, working conditions, training and education, earnings, and job outlook.

O*NET is an ongoing, continually updated system which provides the most up-to-date, comprehensive career and job information available in the U.S. However, it takes a little time to learn and navigate. To start, you can type in any general field, industry, or specific occupation in the Occupation Search box. That will bring up the best occupation matches. You can then click on any of those occupations to get specific information reports on the next screen. The default screen is a *summary* report which includes links to details about the occupation, including wages and employment, job openings, related occupations, and even where you can find training. By clicking on the *detailed report tab*, you can get even more information, often based on what real workers have reported. For instance, under "Context Factors" on the detailed report screen you can see the estimated percent of time workers spend on activities such as working with work groups or teams or being on the telephone.

One of the more interesting features in O*NET is that on the screens just mentioned, there is a section at the top that shows a sample of reported job titles for the occupation you are viewing. An example is the O*NET title Information Technology Project Manager. Job titles employers may use for this occupation are listed as IT Manager, Senior Lead Project Manager, Transition Program Manager, and numerous others. This information is helpful in relating O*NET descriptions with actual jobs listed by employers in job ads.

O*NET also allows you to search for occupations by industry. In other words, if you have an occupation or job in mind, and an interest in working in a specific industry, you can search that industry for jobs. There are also options for advanced searches by personal characteristics, such as skills or interests. To do these types of searches, hover your cursor over "Find Occupations" or "Advanced Search" on the menu bar on the home page of the O*NET website.

Another little-known but very useful resource is the CareerOneStop Business Finder (https://tinyurl.com/ycbfer66). This is a tool for finding employers in any U.S. location who are likely to have jobs in a specific occupation. Just type in the occupation and location. Employers, company information, and contact persons will pop up. This information can tell you where the jobs exist and can be useful in further exploring an occupation using methods discussed below, or even in finding a job.

As you narrow your search, you're probably going to want to know more "real world" information about certain fields and/or jobs. For my client Jack, who thought he would be most suited to becoming a labor relations specialist in the human resources field, the best way to get the inside scoop was to do *informational interviews.* This entails talking directly with people who work in these fields and jobs, and those who teach others.

Informational Interviews

If you decide to do informational interviews, try to set up meetings with those who will give you an objective picture and accurately answer your questions. For instance, let's say you are a maintenance mechanic with a background in installing, troubleshooting, and maintaining industrial equipment. You enjoy that but are interested in a growing field or industry in which you can work outdoors.

After searching O*NET by skills and looking at the list of occupations that came up, you see Solar Thermal Installers and Technicians. One of the sample job titles is Solar Maintenance Technician, designated as a fast-growing occupation. You've heard about these jobs before and now can read about the details in O*NET. The job sounds great, it involves working outdoors, and the salaries are decent, but you need to know more about what it's really like to do this work.

So, you find a local solar energy company and make an appointment to talk with the vice president, who is also a technician. During the meeting, he confirms that it is a growing field, and that you will use your maintenance mechanic skills, but that the job is very physical. It involves climbing on roofs and crawling in bug-infested attics. It can be dangerous. You didn't read much about that aspect, but now that you realize such work could shorten your career or end in severe injury, you decide to consider something else.

When you look for someone with whom to do an informational interview, try to get people you know to make an introduction, or ask contacts from social media such as LinkedIn and Facebook to help. Although making direct contacts with organizations explaining your purpose can also work, getting an introduction can ease the way.

Since you'll want the most objective information possible, be cautious in interviews with those who are trying to recruit you to enter the field (although that can be helpful in a job search), or who have a stake in getting you into a training or education program. It can also be helpful to observe or shadow workers doing their jobs for short periods, if you can get permission during an informational interview.

Internships and Volunteer Work

The next and most direct level of exploration is through internships and volunteer work. Internships may be paid or unpaid, and in many but not all instances may require you to be a student. They afford the opportunity to experience aspects of the job, watch others do it, and interact in environments in which the job is done. The article, "Top Internship Sites" (https://tinyurl.com/y8fu5fwz) describes top websites where you can go to seek internships. You can also try Internships.com.

Volunteer experiences are unpaid and can be done in government and non-profit settings. Opportunities can be found by doing an internet search for "volunteer opportunities," as well as through personal contacts and social media connections.

Getting complete information on potential jobs and careers can be an intensive process. But it will be worth the effort, since career decisions based on good information can save time, effort, and money by avoiding mistakes, and lead to long-term career satisfaction.

Photo by ID 97318901 © Halifah Rahmansyah | Dreamstime.com

PART 4
Landing the Right Job

The following chapters focus on the final step in applying the intersection principle: targeting and getting hired in a job that is consistent with your best skills, your interests, and your best-fit environment.

When attempting to get the right job, targeting is the most crucial part of the process. Only by aiming for the right job in the right place are you likely to most closely approach the "sweet spot," where everything comes together for the greatest sense of passion for and meaning in your work.[11]

As crucial as targeting is, the biggest problem you may face is changing your job-search habits. This can be incredibly difficult. When it comes to looking for a new job, the first instinct is often to go to the internet job boards. After all, there are multitudes of them that have postings for everything, plus career advice and a variety of other services. They're familiar and easy to use. However, the chances of finding a job using job boards is low, usually less than five percent.

Other job listing sources, such as newspaper, magazine, and trade publication ads, are likely to lead to similar results. While it's possible to increase your chances by how you apply—for example, wording in your resume or on the employer's application—you are still likely to be wasting time that could be used more efficiently on a mostly targeted approach.

Contrary to popular wisdom, the same applies to getting leads from your network. Networking is often helpful in getting a new job, but not always a job that will be in your "sweet spot." Targeting requires developing a whole new orientation on how to search, which should also

---

[11]   Much of the material in Part 4 is directly taken or adapted from my earlier book, Simon, S. (2017). *The ultimate job finding solution – A guide to landing a job in the sweet spot of passion and meaningfulness.* Sunnyvale: Pronoun.

enhance your network to include those who can help you with getting the right job in the right place.

CHAPTER 12

Targeting a Job in Your Best Fit Environment

Photo by Rawpixel

Finding a Better Workplace Fit

Jose was a new college graduate with a dual major in biology and sociology. His first job was in a veterinary lab at a university doing tests on blood samples.

He learned the job easily but found that his interests were very dissimilar to the other lab techs. He was a very social person and was also most concerned about how some animals were mistreated. He was becoming more and more isolated from his peers whose conversations focused on analytic methods and the mathematical calculations of what they were doing. He didn't seem to have anything in common with them.

Jose eventually left for an entry-level caseworker job in a local non-profit where he felt much more in sync with his fellow workers and their concerns about helping clients.

Janet was executive assistant to a national program manager in a large government agency. She was highly skilled, but had ongoing conflicts with her boss, which resulted in angry outbursts and a toxic work relationship. She was eventually transferred to a similar job with a supervisor who appreciated her work style and expectations. She thrived in this atmosphere and was subsequently promoted successively, eventually reaching the program manager level.

Targeting first for best-fit environment avoids the inefficiency of searching for opportunities which may or may not be in the right place.

Bob was an assistant professor of computer science at a state university. He loved his field and was a good instructor but could not adjust to the professional conflicts and competitive environment of a university academic department.

He did not get tenure after four years and left for a job in a progressive city library system where he coordinated and taught classes in innovative technology. This was a relaxed and comfortable environment where Bob could be creative and use his best skills in working with his students.

The library was very appreciative of his work since his program and his grant-writing skills helped bring in additional funds to the system to expand technology learning programs.

In these instances, it is evident that the original work environments were not good fits. Fortunately for these workers, changes had a significant impact on restoring meaning and satisfaction to their work, and in the cases of Bob and Janet, their employers benefited significantly as well.

Why Target for Environmental Fit?

If you're looking for work that will result in a sense of passion and meaning over the long term, a *best-fit environment* is one of the four crucial components required according to the intersection principle described in chapter 7. The other components are a job that uses your strongest *skills* as well as your strongest *interests*, and finally the corresponding job *opportunities*.

Targeting the opportunities starts with locating the best-fit work settings that have the type of jobs for which you are searching. Then you can focus your job search only on those organizations. The goal is to seek the work you like and do best in a place where you will feel comfortable, satisfied, and appreciated.

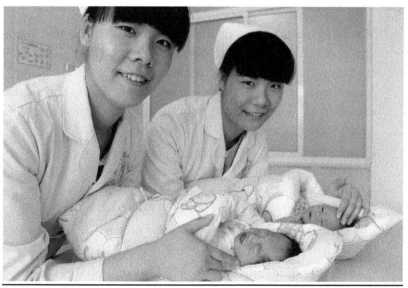

Photo by 66150062xws

Targeting first for best-fit environment avoids the inefficiency of searching for opportunities which may or may not be in the right place. For example, if you conduct your search by looking only for job openings, as most job seekers do, you have a random chance of finding one in your best-fit environment. Furthermore, you will be applying for jobs in many organizations where the fit will not be good enough for you to stay long-term, even if you are given an offer.

By targeting environment first, you are likely to keep your focus exactly in the direction of a win-win situation for you and an employer. You've already assured the fit. So when you get an offer, it will be in the "sweet spot," and the employer finds an employee who fits well and is passionate about his or her work.

This targeting strategy can be particularly effective for you and for employers when the economy is experiencing full employment. For example, in the post-recession 2017 market, if you are in a skilled occupation, employers may be having difficulty filling jobs and certainly in finding applicants who will be in the sweet spot for passion and meaning with a job in their organization. When such applicants present themselves, the company can hit the hiring jackpot.

Assessing Your Best Fit Environment

So, what are the major components of a best-fit environment?

1. **Similarity of interests to the people with whom you work.** This was a major issue with Jose. The match doesn't have to be exact, but it helps if you are generally on the same wavelength. Assessment of your interests using the Holland categories, described in chapter 9, can help identify job environments in which your interests will be similar to others.

2. **Comfort with the organization's culture.** From a best-fit perspective, culture can be viewed as the sum of an organization's values, attitudes, the way people communicate, the way it does business with the public, the way it treats employees and how it gets the work done. Consider your preferences and feelings regarding these questions:

   • Is leadership mainly top-down or bottom-up? Top-down systems tend to depend on structured work, standard rules and procedures, and a strong chain of command. Government organizations often fit this picture. Small businesses with owners who make most decisions can also fit this style, at least in terms of leadership behavior. A bottom-up style assigns more decision making, planning, and autonomy to individuals and collaborative teams. It also relies less on procedural formality.

This style is more valuable where creativity is needed in getting the work done. Organizations can be top-down, but still have departments or units with bottom-up styles. It's helpful to know what the style is in the unit where you might work, as well as throughout the entire organization.

- What is the expectation regarding work hours for the type of job you seek? Is the unwritten norm to work long hours or to stay within a fixed daily schedule? Does the culture allow for flexible work hours and work places (e.g., home)?
- How much value is placed on individual creativity?
- What is the organization's "true" attitude about customers? Some organization say the customer comes first, but behavior of employees may not reflect that commitment.
- Are internal and external communications honest?
- How much does the organization stress ethical and fair behavior?
- What are the organization's attitudes toward diversity? Just looking around or looking at pictures on a website can give you some clues.
- If workers are or become disabled, is the organization friendly to accommodating? This can be significant if you are an older worker with some decline in functioning or health, or if you have an obvious or hidden illness or disability that could impact on absences or need for you to do the work differently than others. Are you likely now, or in the future, to need some accommodations? For example, if you've had a cancer diagnosis in the past, have a heart condition, or have degenerative back and neck conditions, will you be able to get extra time off for medical appointments or surgeries, or have simple accommodations such as a sit-stand desk? Organizations are typically more or less amenable to such things.
- Is there a "profit at all costs" mentality?
- Does the organization keep its commitments to employees?
- To what extent do organization politics govern decisions?

3. **Fit with work team(s),** the people with whom you will work most closely. There can be one or many. Teams can be a group of peers with whom you work collaboratively; a group of customers, managers, and stakeholders; the workers you lead; or a

group of peer managers. In our examples, fit with the primary work team was an issue for Jose and Bob.

Consider the following and your concerns regarding a specific job in an organization:

- Who will be on your work teams?
- Will you be able to communicate constructively with team members?
- Will your skills and personality earn you respect of the other members?
- Will people listen to your ideas?
- Will you be able to lead a team or have a chance of assuming a leadership role?
- Will your interests and work goals be similar to other team members?
- How is competitiveness valued with respect to collaboration and cooperation?
- How is conflict handled?
- If you're looking for promotions, will you be able to compete with the best in your work groups?
- Will you have "star" or "average" potential?
- What is the level of trust within work teams? Will you feel a need to "watch your back"?

4. **Comfort with nature and style of supervision.** This was a problem for Janet. Consider these factors when exploring or interviewing for a specific job:

- Can you expect the supervisor to have a style under which you have thrived before? As we saw with Janet, her first supervisor's style with respect to hers was a nightmare. When she changed jobs, the situation did a 180-degree turn due to more compatible styles.
- Does your prospective supervisor have a positive reputation among current and former employees? When a supervisor is universally viewed negatively, it's a potential red flag.
- Does the prospective supervisor have the trust of and a good reputation among other managers? This is important if you will be coordinating with different departments in your job. It could also impact your ability to be considered for future internal promotions.

- Will the prospective supervisor be the one who decides to hire you? *This can be very significant.* For example, due to a personnel downsizing, a recent client, Pamela, was assigned to a different school in the same system. Previously, she was always a satisfactorily performing teacher, but was transferred due to lack of seniority. At the outset, the principal of the new school explained (to her) that she was not his choice and that he did not want the reassignment. Further, the principal was critical of her work from the outset and throughout the school year. The relationship quickly became contentious. Finally, the principal did not renew her contract.
- Will your supervisor have full decision-making authority, including about future promotions? This was obviously significant in Pamela's case, where the principal could non-renew a teaching contract without review.
- Is this supervisor likely to stay in the job for a while?

5. **Industry fit.** If you have worked in an industry before, such as healthcare, manufacturing, or hospitality, and liked it, you are likely to feel more confidence and comfortable with your overall knowledge of a business in that industry. When Bob made his successful change, he moved out of the university setting, but into a library system. This kept him within the education industry where he was most comfortable.

6. **Physical environment.** Some of us are very aware of the comfort and status of our workplace. If this is the case, will such

factors as the physical location of the facility, the work space you will be assigned, e.g., office size, cubicle, open space among others, or ease in accommodating to disability make a difference? On the surface, this could look like a minor consideration, but not if you've experienced or observed the power scrambles that can take place for an office with a window, or a corner office!

Photo by 12019

7. **Company size.** In what size organization will you feel most comfortable?

When doing an environmental best-fit analysis, list those aspects of the above components and other factors that come to mind that will support your ability to optimize your best skills and interests. Then make them essential criteria of your targeted job search.

Doing the Research

You can start by using personal knowledge or the CareerOneStop Business Finder (https://tinyurl.com/ycbfer66) to locate employers who hire people in your occupation or job of choice. LinkedIn also has several automated features that can quickly expand your list. You might want to start with reading the article by Patrick J. Burns, "LindedIn: It's Still Magic" (https://tinyurl.com/y6uluonl), which will help you understand how to use them.

You may also be able to identify companies from personal or social media contacts, or from talking to colleagues in your field. Finally, you can look to see where jobs in your field are located by using popular job search websites. *These are good for locating companies, but not necessarily for getting jobs.* As discussed in chapter 13, for the actual job search, we encourage focusing on the hidden job market so that you are in the smallest possible pool of applicants and don't waste time on low yield job board searches.

The next step is finding out which of the organizations you identified offers a best-fit environment for you. You can get some information from company websites and then reviews, ratings, and comments from online sources such as Glassdoor (https://tinyurl .com/yd3fgh6l) and The Muse (https://tinyurl.com/ybf64hu8).

Use this information cautiously, since it may be biased. For example, company websites are likely to reflect an organization in a very positive manner. On the other hand, reviews on a website like Glassdoor do not include a representative sample of employees or others. Additionally, the reviews may also be outdated.

Another approach is to use LinkedIn to either contact existing connections or to establish new connections with people who work for the organization. Then, try to arrange a meeting over a cup of coffee to discuss the company. This approach can also lead to direct introductions to hiring managers if you find the organization to be a good fit and you make a good impression on the connection.

Obviously, if you know people who work for the organization, those individuals should be tapped for information as well. Using LinkedIn to develop good connections and develop them into productive relationships is covered thoroughly and succinctly in the article referenced earlier in this section.

Finally, you can simply observe an organization yourself. Sometimes you can find out a lot about the environment by having access to working areas. This is easiest in retail environments, like department stores, where you can publicly observe how employees interact among themselves, with supervisors, and with customers.

Once you decide, from your research, which organizations look like a good fit, before you do the final assessment of environment you will need to locate jobs and be offered interviews in the organizations you choose. This is covered in chapter 13.

The final test of best-fit environment will come during interviews. A potential employer will want to know whether you fit, and for a serious targeted search, you will want to know the same. So, this is an appropriate time ask questions.

Again, you will want to be cautious in evaluating the information, since the interviewer may be looking to paint the rosiest picture. However, you can always diplomatically ask for examples.

If the interviewer talks about the great teamwork atmosphere, you can ask about a particular team and how they worked together to accomplish an important project. Also, if the employer shows serious interest in hiring you, ask to speak with others in the area where you would work.

Shadowing, Internships, and Volunteer Work

These three strategies are discussed in chapter 11 with respect to finding out more information about jobs. They are also the best way of finding out about a best-fit environment, since you can work or observe directly inside the organization, and a potential employer can observe your work and fit as well.

Unfortunately, when searching directly for a job, you're not likely to be able to do any of these things. However, if you are entering a new profession requiring an internship or practicum, you may have the opportunity to select your site.

For example, if you are re-training to be a teacher, professional counselor, social worker, or psychologist, you will need to have at least one field experience, and sometimes several. Unless you are assigned without choice, these can provide pre-employment opportunities to research and select a potential best-fit environment and then to test it out experientially.

Field experiences often lead to employment, so this is a good chance to start out in the right work setting.

Putting It All Together

There are four key points in targeting:

1. Know the job you are searching for.

2. Locate employers in your desired geographical area who have those types of jobs.

3. Self-assess what's most important to you in a work environment.

4. Research the organizations you find and keep your focus on seeking out jobs only in those organizations that offer as close to a best-fit environment for you as possible.

This doesn't mean you won't look at other possibilities that might come to your attention in other organizations; it means that you will discipline yourself to keep most of your time committed to locating jobs in places you will thrive.

Once you get interviews, do the final assessment of how well you fit based on what you learn from interviewers and from interactions with employees. Certainly, if you have opportunities and time for shadowing, internships, or volunteer work, these can be the most revealing methods of discovering where you might fit best.

To help with organizing information on your best-fit environment, use the worksheets in Appendix B of this book. Make copies of the blank worksheets and use one set for each organization under consideration.

CHAPTER 13

Targeting and Finding Hidden Jobs

Jason and George—Different Job Search Strategies

Now that you've targeted the organizations, how do you locate the job(s) you want?

Jason and George are looking for jobs as website designers. Both have had at least 10 years of experience in IT and 7–10 years in designing websites. Neither has had a pristine, continuous work history, but both have good skills and enjoy what they do. Both lost their last jobs due to company cutbacks.

Jason has approached job-seeking by spending most time applying for jobs on popular job boards and on those where jobs specific to website developers and designers are found. He has also gotten some leads from website developers he's worked with. He knows what he wants and has applied for about 75 jobs in three months. He's gotten three first interviews but no job offers.

George has taken a more targeted approach. Based on his research, he first identified companies that would be a good fit for him. He has always been most successful when working alone with clients but leaving the marketing to someone else. He excels in designing medical practice sites and needs the flexibility to work wherever and whenever he feels creative.

He does not like to work on teams, so a small company which assigns designers full responsibility for their projects is best for him. Once he narrowed down the companies that were the best fit, he used strategies to locate existing or potential openings in those companies only. He got two interviews within the first three weeks of looking and was offered both jobs.

George was essentially tapping into the hidden job market. These are jobs that are not widely advertised. This keeps the competition more manageable.

As George found out, this approach not only kept him focused on places where he could best function and thrive, it bypassed the inefficiency of what Jason did: applying for jobs that everyone else was seeking. Jason was essentially in the middle of all the traffic, competing with everyone else, while George was in the passing lane. This is a problem I often see when clients contact me for assistance with a job search that is going nowhere.

Finding the Hidden Jobs

Some hidden jobs may come to your attention through networking contacts, but others can come from tapping into direct channels less used by typical job seekers.

Note that estimates suggest around 50% of job seekers find a job through their network. For targeted searching, your network can certainly be important, but it's not everything. In fact, in initially finding the jobs to apply for or directly getting interviews, more direct methods can sometimes be more efficient. Not being a particularly outgoing person, this is what George did.

Using direct channels can also be particularly useful if you have a limited or no functioning employment network. For example, Lila, a 39-year-old stay at home mom needed to find a job quickly after a financially devastating divorce. She had three years of experience as a human resources specialist in the pharmaceutical industry through her early 30s until she left to raise her two small children. At 39, although she wanted to return to similar work, she had no active employment network to help with finding a job—or even a LinkedIn account.

So, let's look at the direct channels for finding hidden jobs first; then we'll look at an efficient approach toward starting and using an existing network.

Consider using the following direct methods with your targeted organizations:

1. Check the organization website for posted jobs. Jobs listed here may not be on job boards. That reduces the competition.

2. Using the CareerOneStop Business Finder (https://tinyurl.com/ycbfer66) call one of the contacts listed to ask about jobs, or to try to set up an informational interview with a supervisor or employee who works in a unit that employs people in your specialty. The purpose would be to find out about the organization, the types of work they do, and the nature of specialists they employ. If you are new to the field, you can frame it in terms of your desire to find out more about the types of jobs in the field and what people in those jobs do. The idea is not to request a job interview, but request help with getting information. This is a low-pressure way to get a foot in the door. There

is no pressure on the organization to interview you for a job, but in effect you are being interviewed as much as you are gathering information. Even if there are no job openings, establishing a good relationship results in an inside link that could result in a recommendation for a future job inside or even outside the organization.

3. If you have many years of experience in a profession, or are looking in a very specialized field, and have a strong reputation, consider working with a recruiter who works with the organization. To learn how to find them you can review the infographic at LinkedIn (https://tinyurl.com/khkplyz).

   The problem with recruiters is that they are middlemen/women serving the role of gatekeeper. While they can help you, they can also stop you at the door if they have, or think they can find, a better candidate. So, if you want to penetrate an organization quickly, you take some risk by using a recruiter.

4. Try a more aggressive strategy of getting in the door. The boldest approach is to walk into the company without an appointment and see if a manager is available to talk to you. Take along a resume. Once you're inside and make a connection with someone, you can decide whether to frame your visit in terms of an informational interview or a search for a specific job.

   In very small companies, the first person you see may be the hiring person, so you won't even have to get by an in-house gatekeeper, such as a human resources specialist. In my company, when someone walks in the door, looks professional, and wants information or is looking for a job that I hire, I'm eager to talk to them right away. It may save me a lot of recruitment time now, or later when I'm ready to hire.

   Walking into the company is a high success probability strategy because you can often get there when the timing is right to pique the employer's interest. It's the ultimate approach to tapping the hidden job market. Richard Bolles, in repeated editions of *What Color is Your Parachute?* cites this as being among the highest yield methods in quickly getting a job.[12]

5. Most job searches, including a targeted search, can become more effective with networking. However, it's important to network

---

12   Bowles, R. N. (2016). *What Color is Your Parachute?* New York: Ten Speed Press.

efficiently and judiciously. Otherwise networking can take up more time than it's worth. Here are some networking essentials to consider when doing a job search:

- Open a LinkedIn account if you don't already have one. Aside from networking purposes, your presence on LinkedIn will be important for other reasons. *Fully and accurately complete your profile* with no errors and no exaggerations. Treat this with the same care as your resume. Then start requesting to connect with other LinkedIn members that you know and trust, and judiciously with others you think might be good connections to have if they accept. When you make a connection, if you don't already know them, try to communicate and establish at least a superficial relationship. Connections that will work for you are those with whom you have an actual relationship.

- If you already have a LinkedIn account with a network of connections, try to find those who work for the organizations you are targeting. If you know the connection, ask if they can introduce you to a manager or other hiring official to discuss job opportunities in the organization. If you don't have such connections, find someone within the organization and request to connect. If they accept, communicate something brief about yourself and ask them to do the same. If you can establish ongoing interaction, you might suggest an informal meeting; offer to buy them coffee or breakfast, since you have been looking for a job and would like to find out more about their organization. If they accept and you impress them positively, such a meeting could lead to introductions to people who do hiring in your field.

- For perhaps the quickest way to start and/or develop a LinkedIn network, you can use the latest LinkedIn technology tools. The article by Patrick J. Burns entitled "LinkedIn: It's Still Magic," which I mentioned earlier (https://tinyurl .com/y6uluonl), written for career services professionals offers a short, easy to follow summary of how to build a LinkedIn network, expand it, and use it effectively for targeting purposes with the tools LinkedIn offers as of 2017. *Note: such tools could change or advance further in the future.*

- Talk to friends, relatives, and colleagues with whom you have a positive relationship. Let them know you are looking for a job and ask for their help. Tell them the type of job you are looking for and the places you would like to work, or at least the type of place.

This is a difficult step for most people who have lost jobs because you are telling people, with whom you've had the status of a successful worker, that you are no longer working. You've lost status and may feel ashamed to admit it, and that you need help. You may feel like you're begging. But, the reality is that most people, when asked, feel good that you came to them. It provides a feeling of importance and being needed, and most people want to do what they can to help.

I've worked with even the highest-level workers in this situation who have been fired or laid off. When the anxiety is overcome to make those first few contacts, the positive results are remarkable!

For many of us, this approach represents a change in how we view ourselves. Our lives have often taught us that we can solve our own problems. We don't need help. That self-concept must change if networking is to be effective.

- If you are in, or anticipate, a difficult and long job search, join a job club. Job clubs bring job seekers together, in a structured setting, to work on finding jobs. I have found such meetings to be among the most effective options because they provide relationship-based connections, new ideas, and input from others' job search experiences. Most importantly, they can provide emotional support during a difficult search, helping to counteract feelings of discouragement and depression. To find a job club, check with your local One Stop Center (https://tinyurl.com/ycgbsfqf), or local non-profit agencies and educational institutions that provide career services.

Once you've identified a job or begun an initial discussion with someone in the organization about an opening or potential opening, you'll need to formally present your qualifications. So, you will either need a resume (or curriculum vitae), and/or you'll need to submit the company's application. Issues regarding applications are covered in chapter 14.

CHAPTER 14

Applying for Jobs

Once you've located a job you want, then what? How do you apply? It sounds like a straightforward process, but if you haven't done it for a while, or if you haven't been successful with your applications, it's probably time to take a look at what you're doing with respect to current thinking.

As a first step, you should be ready with a well-written resume you can submit online or in person. In many instances, an application will be made directly using an employer's application form and other materials online, but the resume is still a fundamental introductory tool.

If you are applying during a personal visit to an employer or doing an informational interview, always bring a resume.

Writing a Basic Resume

A resume is a summary presentation of yourself to a potential employer. The purpose is usually to get an interview. It is suggested that you write a *basic* (generic) resume and save it on your computer. Then modify it to correspond with the specific requirements and terminology in the job announcement when you apply for specific jobs. This will align your qualifications with what the employer needs and make you more likely to be asked to interview.

It is to your advantage to create the content and at least a draft of the *basic* resume yourself, rather than hiring someone to write it. An exception is to hire a professional resume writer who uses techniques that force you to think deeply about your experience, skills, and accomplishments, document them, and then helps you organize the information into resume format.

Going through this in-depth process will serve you well when you do resume modifications, prepare for and have job interviews. If you draft your own resume, you can also use a resume writer or career consultant, to clean up what you've already done and put the resume in a final, most presentable form.

There is no single best way to write a *basic* resume. As a minimum, it should be no longer than one to two pages, typed on standard white paper, must contain NO spelling or grammatical errors, and should grab the reader's attention at the beginning.

Note that the one to two-page limit may not apply if an employer invites you for an interview based on your reputation or a special recommendation. In that case, the interviewer may want a more detailed description of your background, including a curriculum vitae, which is longer and far more detailed. Try to find out what is desired in advance so you'll be prepared. For information on preparing a curriculum vitae, visit https://tinyurl.com/y7rdp9es.

For a basic resume, include:
1. **Your identifying information,** i.e., name, address (optional), city, state, a non-work phone number, and a non-work, professional-sounding email address. For example, have an email address like ssmith364@gmail.com rather than using ilovemycat@gmail.com. Also include a link to your LinkedIn

profile if you have one. If you do that, make sure your LinkedIn profile is fully updated.

2. **A branding statement at the beginning of the resume.** This very briefly explains the value you can bring to an organization. Read "How To Add a Branding Statement to Your Resume" (https://tinyurl.com/y7njtyeu) for a credible source with further explanation and examples. A career summary state-ment (https://tinyurl.com/y8nc7vaw), which might be a few lines longer, can substitute for the briefer branding statement. However, it too should focus on your value to an organization. The critical element in either of these statements is grabbing the reader's attention by demonstrating *not what you want,* but what value you bring.

3. **Information about your current and past jobs over the last 10 years,** with a focus on your quantified achievements. When listing jobs, do so in reverse chronological order.

4. **Your education** in reverse chronological order.

5. **Other sections if pertinent to strengthen your qualifica-tion profile and differentiate you from other candidates.** These include detailed skills, military service, professional or other affiliations, and extracurricular activities. However, do not include anything irrelevant to the jobs for which you will be applying.

The use of job objectives in resumes is no longer usually considered desirable because they focus on what you want rather than what you can do for an employer. However, if you have a very specific or specialized job objective, or if you are changing to a new career, you can insert a job objective prior to your branding or career summary statement.

There are several basic resume formats you can use depending on your circumstances. These are:

1. **Chronological**—This is the style most preferred by reviewers. It works best when you have a work background with no or few breaks in continuity, and jobs in the same or similar fields. If you use one of the other formats, you may run the risk of an employer sensing that there are "problems" in your work history before even reading further. This is not always the case, but it's worth mentioning. Visit Resume Genius (https://tinyurl

.com/ybh5yoje) for a sample of a well-written chronological resume, as well as other samples for different fields.

2. **Functional**—This is useful if you have gaps in your work history; a lot of short-term jobs, or very little work history; have worked in varied or different fields; or have periods in your life with volunteer or other experiences not associated with paid work, *but that resulted in special skills you want to highlight.* Visit Resume Resource (https://tinyurl.com/yc6r2fr2) for a sample of a well-written functional resume, or Resume Genius (https://tinyurl.com/yc3amoxk) for another. Note that, in these samples, dates of employment are not shown. The issue of gaps in employment is so pervasive that chapter 16 covers that separately with respect to resumes and interviews.

> **In a targeted employment search, the idea is to keep your eye on the ball: the right job in the right place.**

3. **Combination**—This format creatively combines elements from both the chronological and functional. For this reason, it is a good option if you have a long, continuous job history encompassing different fields, full-time and/or part-time, (e.g., medical practitioner, university professor, chief operating officer of a company). The combination format opens a lot of possibilities.

For example, I like a separate section on Skills or Skills and Achievements, after the brief branding statement or statement of qualifications, but before a chronological statement of jobs. This focuses early in the resume on a detailed statement of what might be most relevant to the employer in selecting an applicant. It serves as a 1–2 punch in the first 5–10 seconds of review.

See the image at Resume Genius (https://tinyurl.com/yczbolgl) for a sample of a combination resume using the skills/achievements option, or Powerful Sample Resume Formats (https://tinyurl.com/rbwq2q) for several more using different creative strategies.

Modifying the Basic Resume

When you are applying with a resume, modify your basic resume to reflect your qualifications as close to the job requirements as possible. Do this honestly, without over- or understating your qualifications.

You'll find the requirements in the job announcement, if there is one, or from any discussions you've had about the job or potential job with someone within the organization. For example, you may have 20 different skills. *For each job for which you apply, modify your basic resume to include only those pertinent to that job.*

Similarly, modify what you emphasize in your statements of experience and achievements to those items that are specific to the stated job requirements. The organization may be using automated resume screening through an *applicant tracking system,* so try to incorporate *exact words* from the statement of job requirements in your resume, when possible. Generally, large companies are most likely to use such systems.

Finally, to maximize effectiveness of your resume, check out this brief article for some basic do's and don'ts in getting your resume noticed (https://tinyurl.com/p24hd45). Make sure you save each modification of the basic resume for potential future use.

Improving Your Chances of Getting an Interview

If you are applying with a resume, you will usually need an accompanying email or *cover letter.* When you transmit information by email, handle this like any other business correspondence, i.e., use *perfect* grammar and spelling, and be concise. Detailed guidelines and samples of cover letters are provided at The Balance (https://tinyurl.com/ycr9spmw).

When you attach a resume, use PDF format, unless a specific software format is requested, such as MS Word. PDF assures that the formatting will remain the same as on the original document when opened, regardless of the software program you used to create the resume. It also does not require the recipient to have that program on their computer.

Following up on selected job applications can improve the chances of getting an interview. Try to identify the hiring manager. Then, use your network on LinkedIn, or through other sources, to attempt to get someone who knows the manager to arrange a meeting for you or at least mention your name to the hiring official. Visit https://tinyurl.com/3p9wtdn for a review of application follow-up strategies.

In a targeted employment search, the idea is to keep your eye on the ball: the right job in the right place. In a search focusing on the hidden job market, you have already narrowed to jobs in the right place, with less competition, than in a general job search. A solid application process should further narrow the competition and increase your chances of getting a job you want.

CHAPTER 15

From Interview to Employment

Photo by Adabara

How Did George Do It?

Looking back at George, the website designer in chapter 13, he used the targeting strategy to find the best-fit work settings and the jobs that were available in those organizations. He then was able to get two job offers very quickly based on his interviews. How did he do it?

Using George as an example, let's look at how you can have an impressive interview—one that leaves *both you and the interviewer* thinking that this is the "sweet spot" job for you and for the organization. We'll look at George's first interview. He used a similar strategy for interviews with the second employer as well.

Preparation, Preparation, More Preparation

George was very detail oriented, and this carried over to his job-search strategy. He had already done a thorough review of the company for best fit. Now he could write a list of questions to clarify some points about that in his interviews. The most important one was whether he would need to work on a formal team or not. He worked best in an atmosphere where he called the shots but had a team of website specialists with whom he could consult as needed.

George found out about the first job through a contact he made at this company, using his LinkedIn connections. Before he applied, he got a copy of a job announcement that had not yet been posted and a position description.

He immediately prepared a revised resume to specifically highlight the five most pertinent skills and achievements he had that matched this job. He sent the resume to the team leader of the group in which the new person would be hired. When he was contacted for the interview, he was able to use his contact again to get some background information about the interviewer that might help in making a connection.

He found that the interviewer was an avid Ohio State football fan, something that George could easily connect with, since he graduated from that school and tried out for the team as a freshman. Finally, prior to the interview, George reviewed all his skills so he would not forget anything, if the occasion arose, to mention something during the interview.

He had recently done a self-assessment of his hidden skills (see chapter 8), partially for use in pre-interview preparation. He also carefully reviewed his resume so he would be able to talk about and expand upon any point that might be raised by the interviewer. He particularly thought about the achievements he included so he could elaborate on how his past experience could help the company bolster its reputation and income.

Based on his preparation, George was able to make a quick connection with the interviewer, get his questions answered to his satisfaction, and clearly make a case for his value to the organization. He got an offer that day, contingent upon a reference check. In fact, from the company's perspective, being able to interview and hire a very qualified candidate before even needing to post the job would save a lot of time and recruitment expense.

It pays to take the time to prepare in detail to give yourself every competitive advantage. The interview will not go exactly as you expect, but you will be ready to make a solid connection with the interviewer and to speak knowledgeably about yourself and about the company. You will know your resume well and be ready to expand on your skills, achievements, and experiences without hesitation.

If you applied based on a targeted job search, you have also done research on the company. Review that and prepare a list of further questions about your fit with the organization environment based on the criteria in chapter 12.

Note that you may have more than one interview before a hiring decision is made. You should prepare similarly for each.

Interview Basics, Questions, and Oddball Questions

For in-person interviews, attire should be consistent with what people in the position typically wear. When in doubt, stay on the conservative side. Grooming, as well as neat and pressed clothes, are essentials.

In George's case, he took the somewhat conservative route because he was told that website people in the organization dressed very informally, but supervisors and managers never wore jeans or t-shirts. George decided to wear a buttoned shirt and neat, casual slacks, but not jeans, shorts or t-shirt for the interview. If the interviewer liked him and decided to introduce him to someone at a higher management level, he wanted to look impressive.

It's best to be on time or slightly early; *never late*! These are all first-impression issues, so pay close attention. For phone or video interviews, make sure your equipment is working properly before the interview. For phone, land-line phones are clearer and more reliable. If you only have a cellphone, be in an area where you get the best reception.

All interviews are different. However, at GlassDoor.com (https://tinyurl.com/y7ctpalr) you'll find the most common interview questions, plus you'll find an article about potential "oddball" questions (https://tinyurl.com/yc2h78mn). When responding to questions, keep your answers brief and focused.

References

Generally, employers will want references from current and former supervisors. Sometimes, if supervisors cannot be given, other managers with whom you have interacted or worked, or colleagues who are familiar with your work will be acceptable. The key issue for prospective employers is getting reliable, objective information from others who have observed you and can evaluate how you perform and behave as an employee. Usually, you should be prepared to provide three to five references.

Make sure you contact each proposed reference in advance to let them know you are applying for jobs and that you would like to use their names as references. Do not use anyone from whom you have not received permission or agreement in advance or who you think might provide damaging information.

Sometimes you may ask someone who agrees, but you get a sense that they are only lukewarm about being a reference. This would be a sign that you might want to move on to someone else. If you are currently employed and do not want your employer to find out that you are job hunting, providing references becomes a sensitive issue. You can assume that if you let any colleagues or others in the organization know you are looking, then the information will eventually get back to your supervisor or other managers. This can be damaging and cause loss of trust, or worse. You could, however, consider using past supervisors from other organizations who have no known contact or association with your current employer, and who you know will keep your search confidential. As an employer, I have found such references to be helpful and sufficient when an applicant needs confidentiality from their current employer.

The best-case scenario is to be able to discuss your intentions with your boss before starting your job search. However, if this isn't feasible, the situation can be discussed during job interviews. If alternatives are not available, the potential employer should be asked to maintain confidentiality and only check references, with your permission, at the time a job offer is seriously being considered. At that point, if you can be informed and you are ready to take the risk for the job in question, you can approach your supervisor and contact your other references. You may want to ask for a signed offer letter first from the prospective employer with the understanding that if the information from references is not acceptable, then the job offer would be withdrawn. If you are seriously looking for a new job, at some point your employer is going to need to know.

Salary and Negotiation

A common question I get is "How do I deal with salary in an interview?" It's usually best to wait until the interviewer is ready to bring this up, meaning that you are being given serious consideration for the job. If you bring it up, particularly before the interviewer is sure you are a leading candidate, you can give the wrong impression and disqualify yourself.

As a general rule, if you choose to raise the issue of salary before your prospective employer does, save it for last, at the time you and the employer are sold on each other. Visit InterviewCoach .com (https://tinyurl.com/ydf22y9h) for an article on questions an employer might ask about salary and how you might respond.

Once you have an offer, then you are in a position to, and should, negotiate reasonably. You've already been offered the job, so you know you're the candidate they want. Negotiation is usually expected and will not result in withdrawal of the offer, unless the meeting becomes contentious.

In fact, if done effectively, negotiation could result in substantially more than the original offer. For purposes of negotiation, you will need to understand the complete salary and benefits package. If you can't negotiate more salary, you may be able to negotiate more benefits, such as additional vacation time and full payment of medical insurance premiums.

For negotiation purposes, you should know the salary range for similar jobs. You can use such sites as salary.com, payscale.com, and glassdoor.com to find information. When negotiating salary, shoot for the point in the usual salary range you think your background, experience, and expectations fit best.

If you think it's on the high end or above the salary range, be ready to present the supporting data. Data-based negotiation can be very convincing and reasonable, as long as you are within what the organization is willing and able to pay. For example, I once did a salary negotiation for a university job that netted well above what was expected to be paid for a temporary assistant professor. The negotiation was based on data I was able to present about my salary history in non-university positions. Use whatever data you can to make your case.

Post Interview Follow-Up

Write a *thank you note* as soon as you complete each interview. This is an important touch and can distinguish you from other candidates. There are several alternatives for doing this. Some experts recommend a standard "snail mail" letter. Others suggest that a handwritten note to each person involved in the interview process can make the difference in selecting among a few qualified candidates. There is always the option of an email message.

Dear Dr. Hole,

Thank you for the opportunity to meet with you yesterday. It was a thrill to meet someone who is as much of a CE junkie as I am. Your approach to using seaweed as a restorative agent is fascinating. I look forward to hearing from you.

Holly Hygienist, BS, RDH

Source expensereported.com

You will need to assess the method that will best fit the interviewer and situation. For example, for a phone interview, an email may be most appropriate. For a personal interview or series of contacts, the handwritten note option might be most productive.

Whichever method you choose, be sure you have the correct address(es) that will get the correspondence directly to the right people. Additional follow-up suggestions are presented in the article titled, "A Guide to Juggling Multiple Job Offers and Coming Out on Top," (https://tinyurl.com/y7wbt4rd) including information on sample thank you letters and more intensive contact activities.

Considering Job Offers

After several successful interviews, George got two job offers within a week. This put him in somewhat of a bind, albeit a happy one! He had to make a relatively quick decision.

Whether you have a single offer or multiple ones, it's worthwhile to evaluate whether the job will truly fit the criteria for finding passion and meaning over the long term. There are several factors to consider.

First, is this job truly consistent with my best skills, and of those, the ones I am most interested in using, my general work interests, and my best-fit work environment? If the job meets those criteria, you have a great fit and can be expected to find passion and meaning. If the job partially meets the criteria, consider whether there may be other offers coming that may be a better fit. This was the situation with George. He had a few days to decide on the first offer, and the next interview was coming up a day later.

In some instances, a compromise is worthwhile. For example, in George's case, the first job was a great fit, as was the company culture and the work team. However, the location was a little farther than was practical to travel every day, the salary was a little lower than he expected, and he would work out of a cubicle rather than a private office. The second job was not as good a fit overall, but the salary was slightly higher. Here, he would also work out of a cubicle.

Over the long term, the intrinsic rewards of the work you are doing, such as a sense of accomplishment and competence, will probably make you feel very good about yourself and your contribution.

The extrinsic factors, like salary and work spaces, can change over time, and while important, may ultimately not generate the sense of passion and well-being that a meaningful job can provide. So, for George, the compromise in taking the first job might have been worthwhile.

Second, will the job and/or industry allow for growth over time? For George, both jobs were in the IT industry, so this was not an issue.

Third, how will the job impact the rest of my everyday life—what I do on weekends, how might it affect my spouse and family, what are the implications for child care, and overall stress? George knew that the longer commute for the first job would require driving an hour more per workday and would put more mileage on his car. There would be increased costs of gasoline, as well as for child care, since his wife worked later hours, and less overall time with the family.

How did this all work out for George? First, his situation required some juggling and delay tactics to avoid prematurely accepting the first job, which was a great fit but had some drawbacks. He really didn't want to do the extra travel, which would be costly and interfere with family responsibilities. However, he didn't want to lose this opportunity if he failed to get an offer from the next interview, or if the job or terms were not as good.

So, since he only had a verbal offer from the first employer, he requested a written offer. He knew that would take a few days, especially since the offer was contingent upon a reference check. A written offer is necessary anyway to document that the job offer was made and to state the terms of employment. If you get into a situation where you need to use such delay tactics, this article titled, "A Guide to Juggling Multiple Job Offers and Coming Out on Top!" (https://tinyurl.com/yandhb5c) at theMuse.com covers a variety of strategies that may help.

What finally happened? George did get an offer after the interview for the second job. However, he really wanted the first job. Once he got the written offer, and before rejecting the second job, he contacted the interviewer from the first job, told him he really wanted to accept, but explained his concerns. As a result, he was able to negotiate a 10% higher salary to cover his added travel expenses.

In addition, he got a verbal commitment from the new supervisor that after about three months, assuming everything was going well, he would be able to work from home two to three days per week. Based on the interview and the content of the offer letter, George judged that the company really thought he would be a great asset. He felt comfortable carefully negotiating for the additional salary and work-at-home time without jeopardizing the offer.

Thank You, Thank You

If you reject an offer, send a thank you note, and show your appreciation for the offer. Say good things about the company and the interviewer(s). This enhances your reputation and, you never know, it may pay dividends in the future. It's always good when people remember you in a positive light.

It's also good policy to send thank you notes to the interviewer(s) at the job you accepted. You can let each one know how much you look forward to working for the company and with them. This starts you off on a highly positive note.

After considering and acting on the above, you should end up with the right job, one that falls within that sweet spot of passion and meaningfulness. You should also have an employer who can look forward to an excited and highly motivated new employee—clearly what we all want, a win-win situation.

CHAPTER 16

Dealing with Gaps in Employment

Photo by sasint

Significance of Employment Gaps

The need to manage gaps in employment has become quite common, one of the most frequent issues I see with those seeking a new job. So, if that's happening to you, you're not alone. In fact, in reviewing thousands of employment histories, I've found it more common to find short and/or long gaps than not.

Gaps in employment do not necessarily mean an employer will eliminate you from consideration. Employers are usually most concerned with filling jobs with the most qualified applicant. However, if someone has gaps in their job history, that may raise a flag about why, or concerns about implications for attendance, performance, longevity, or other workplace problems. For example, as an employer I always worry about anything that could mean a "high maintenance" employee which is time-consuming and expensive for the organization.

On the other hand, as both an employer and a professional career counselor, I know those concerns can often be proactively and successfully addressed by an applicant both in the resume and in any interviews that follow. Typical gap issues that can be acceptably explained are inability to find a new job after a layoff, need to take time out to care for a sick relative, taking years off to raise children, leaving a job to find something more satisfying, or an unsuccessful attempt at starting a business.

If the issues are serious or high risk, such as frequent job losses due to inability to do the job or adjust to normal work demands, chronic psychiatric illness, substance abuse, alcohol dependence, or incarceration for a felony, the impact on a traditional job search becomes more significant. In those cases, your job search will likely take longer or may show better results by enlisting the help of a public or non-profit agency, or private rehabilitation counselor who can help with job adjustment issues and personally find a willing employer.

Managing Gaps in Resumes and Cover Letters

For most people who have employment gaps, honesty, with an emphasis on strengths, skills, and positive explanations is a good way to approach the employment search. There is really no sense in trying to lie or exaggerate. Most employers will eventually find out and your credibility will be ruined, not to mention the possibility of getting fired later for lying if you should get a job.

When writing your resume, a functional format as discussed in chapter 14, can deal with gaps by placing the focus on your strengths in terms of experience, skills, and achievements. For example, the key structural parts might be your Qualifications Summary, Experience, and Employment. Under Experience, there might be three functional categories such as *Customer Service, Sales,* and *Administration.* Under each functional category you would describe the major tasks you have performed, special achievements, and any related special skills you have. In the Employment section separately list employers, position held, and dates.

With regard to dates of employment, if you have one or more short gaps, you can list years rather than specific dates. For example, if you worked January, 2011–October, 2012, then did not work again until March, 2013, you could use a yearly format. For the first job you would use 2011–2012 as the dates of employment and 2013 as the date for the second job. If you use that format, be consistent for all your jobs. Any gaps or overlaps within those

For most people who have employment gaps, honesty, with an emphasis on strengths, skills, and positive explanations is a good way to approach the employment search.

years can then be explained in an interview if it comes up.

If you have longer gaps or gaps that don't fit a continuous work history using the yearly format, you can include the dates in the yearly format under Employment, but give a short, concise explanation of the gap, e.g., "2007–2008—was caring for my elderly, ill parents." You could also elaborate further in the cover letter.

If the reason for the gap is due to something that could be viewed with a negative stereotype such as criminal behavior or psychiatric hospitalization, then use a statement in the resume such as "will explain in interview" or "see explanation in cover letter." If it is something that can best be explained positively in an interview, then use the "will explain in interview" option in the resume rather than take the greater risk of pre-interview elimination because of too much elaboration in the cover letter. If the gaps are short and in the distant past, for example, nine years ago followed by continuous employment, there is usually no need to explain in the resume or cover letter.

Explaining Gaps in Interviews

For the interview, plan and practice in advance to answer questions about employment gaps. This is when employers will have the best opportunity to personally assess your credibility and honesty. So in explaining your employment gaps you will likely need to walk a line of giving an honest version of the gap presented in a manner that seems reasonable to the interviewer, while showing that what you did during the gap either enhances your attractiveness for the job, or at the very least, is not a barrier. Whether the reasons for the gap are easy to explain or not, discuss them in the context of any positives that have resulted from that period. Include any part-time work or volunteer activities, community service, training courses and workshops you attended. This shows that you were active, enhancing your skills, and doing constructive activity.

In summary, when it comes to dealing with employment gaps, the key concept is to explain honestly in a positive context while mostly stressing the assets that you can bring to the job and organization. Planning well for this will enhance your credibility during the interview and the probability of overcoming any negative impacts of past unemployment.

CHAPTER 17

Age: How Much Does It Matter?[13]

Photo by Maryland GovPics

I t's very common to hear someone in their 50s or 60s, unemployed or considering a change in job or career, express concerns about being unable to find work because of age. To what extent is that a valid concern and if so, what can be done about it?

---

[13]   This chapter was co-authored by Steven Simon, Ph.D. and Elise Prezant.

When it comes to age and work, it's usually not a simple matter of "age discrimination," as many of us often assume. If you have concerns about age, it's usually one of a constellation of factors impacting on whether or how easily you will find a job. If the other factors are dealt with, then the impact of age is diminished, or can become a non-issue.

Aging and An Unexpected Need to Work

Terri, 55, had been married for nearly 30 years when her husband suddenly told her he wanted a divorce and was moving out of state. Although she had an accounting degree, Terri had not worked since her two children were born over 20 years ago. She always assumed that once her children were out on their own, she and her husband would be enjoying their "golden" years together.

When Terri came in for career counseling, she was still dealing with all the legal and emotional ramifications of the divorce. However, she was also beginning to realize that she had to find a way to support herself. Terri's attorney felt that she would eventually receive financial support from her soon-to-be ex-husband, but how much and when was at the mercy of the legal system.

Terri was, understandably, overwhelmed with the prospect of looking for a job. She hadn't worked outside the home in many years, knew that her accounting skills were outdated, her work "network" nonexistent, and she was already in her mid-50s. Terri also had no idea how to even begin her job search. On top of all these concerns, she knew from other members of her "Suddenly Single" group that even if she found a job, it needed to offer enough flexibility, for at least one or two years, to allow her to be available for all divorce proceedings on short notice. So, as you can see, in Terri's case, while age could be a concern, outdated skills, lack of up-to-date job-seeking skills, almost no established network to help, and personal issues that would impact on job reliability and performance were more likely to prevent her from getting a job.

Terri's story is not unusual. Whether it's due to divorce, death of a spouse, or job loss for someone who is single, many women in their 50s and 60s find themselves in a position of suddenly, often unexpectedly, needing to support themselves and sometimes their families, even including aging parents. As career counselors, we are mindful of the recent trauma these women have gone through and generally inquire about and/or recommend mental health counseling. The job search process is stressful enough for someone who is aging and emotionally healthy, with a good support system.

For women like Terri who are already on an emotional roller coaster, facing the regular and expected rejections all aging job seekers face can be paralyzing. Once she gets a job, she will also have to deal with the impact of her personal issues on being a reliable employee. In addition to seeking professional mental health counseling, see Part 6, "Managing the Emotions of a Difficult Job Search," and Part 9, "Recognizing and Managing Emotional Dysfunction at Work," for other coping strategies.

> **When it comes to age and work, it's usually not a simple matter of "age discrimination," as many of us often assume.**

Work After a Late-Career Layoff or Termination

Earl, a former client, married with grown children, was age 64 at the time we first met in 2014. He had an advanced degree in business and 30 years of experience in the finance industry. He lost his last job as a bank executive when the financial markets collapsed in 2008. He did some occasional substitute teaching after the layoff but viewed himself as essentially unemployed for six years.

He had some savings and investments but wanted more income and desperately wanted to return to a job with what he viewed as suitable status. He could not find an executive-level job, or even get interviews, and was not willing to consider anything totally different, at a lower level, or that he considered "menial." He thought he was being discriminated against mainly because of his age. Earl was not an inherently social person, nor did he ever develop strong relationships with colleagues that he believed could help him. Although he had 500 connections on LinkedIn, he couldn't think of a single one that he wanted to ask for assistance with his job search.

As with Earl, clients often focus on age as a primary concern, even sometimes those as young as in their late 40s. If you are having difficulty finding a job in your 50s, 60s, or beyond, there may be more of a tendency to attribute that to age. We've heard, "I'm pretty sure I'm being discriminated against because of my age," "Employers want workers half my age. They can pay them less," "I have more experience than the supervisors who are interviewing me, and I know more than them." Some of the statements reflect reality, but some reflect attitudes that could serve as barriers to being successful on a job.

Age Can Work Both Ways

Age can be a liability or an asset. For example, if you haven't worked in many years and can't use computers, modern office hardware, basic software, and know nothing about cloud-based applications, you'll probably be viewed as a "dinosaur" by a potential employer. It's not just your age, it's how well you've kept up with technology, the engine that runs modern business. If you believe that you know better than your potential boss or other workers about how the work should be done or project an attitude of "this job is below me," you risk being viewed as an older person who will resist learning new things.

On the other hand, if you strongly demonstrate skills and achievements that can add value more than other applicants because of your extensive work background, and you have evidence and an attitude that shows you're always eager to learn and improve, then age becomes an asset. You project *maturity* and *stability*, not being antiquated and over the hill.

Mature, knowledgeable employees serve as vital role models in a younger, less stable workforce. For example, if you're a sports fan, you can see the importance of older, seasoned players in a locker room, even if their playing skills are now diminished. Skills and important attitudes can be transmitted by mature workers in a way that can't be duplicated by younger employees.

Your assets can come through to a potential employer at first by how you structure your resume, and subsequently in interviews. Other factors could intervene, such as health and projected longevity, but overall, employers want value. If you can unequivocally show that, any employer prejudices about age should be reduced or eliminated. Start with your resume, using the guidelines in Chapter 14.

Overcoming the Barriers

For Terri, it was initially important that she understood how the job search process today was markedly different from the process she recalled from 20 years ago. Her job search plan was broken down into smaller steps that she was more able to confidently tackle each week. Terri's plan included:

1. **Developing a list of contacts.** It was important that Terri not make any assumptions about who she "thought" would be in a position to help. While she didn't have many, if any, work related contacts, Terri certainly knew many people in her community such as friends, neighbors, relatives, people she volunteered with in several local organizations, and members of her synagogue. She didn't forget casual contacts like store clerks, cleaning people, doctors, and others who she saw briefly but regularly. Terri agreed that she did not know everyone these individuals knew, and some of them might be able to provide solid advice, suggestions or even job leads.

2. **Creating a LinkedIn profile and being an active user.** LinkedIn offers a wealth of information and resources to job seekers, but to be most visible to recruiters and hiring managers it is necessary to be active on it, not just amass a large number of connections. This means regularly "liking" posts, following target companies, commenting on articles, posing questions to groups and even writing blogs in areas of expertise. Terri was able to make time to work on LinkedIn at least one hour a day.

3. **Assessing physical appearance.** This is not an easy topic to discuss, but the reality of getting older is that younger people often see older workers as even older than they are, and these younger people are now more likely to be the ones conducting the interviews. With that comes many misconceptions: older workers have less energy, get sick more often, haven't kept up with technology—you get the idea. Therefore, it is important

that job seekers make every effort to appear as young as they feel. This may include updating your wardrobe and hairstyle, having the newest technology, i.e., an up-to-date smartphone, and getting into or staying in shape. Like it or not, looks and first impressions do matter.

4. **Considering contract or temporary positions.** In this "gig" economy, Terri needed to realize that she was just as likely to find a short-term or temporary position and that could work for her as well. This would give her a chance to brush up on her skills, have something current to add to her resume and most importantly, help her pay some bills.

5. **Not overlooking small to mid-size companies.** Although Terri didn't have recent accounting experience, she had a great deal of life experience, volunteer and community experience and other interests and passions. Smaller companies are more likely to value these skills, personal experiences, and personality traits more than larger companies.

6. **Considering that younger hiring managers may feel insecure about hiring someone who is older and more experienced.** As we get older, we can legitimately say "at this stage of my life I am" *fill in the blank*: "no longer interested in having your level of responsibility"; and finally, "confident that I can make you look good."

So, how does Terri's story end? Through a personal contact, Terri was able to land a part-time position as a bookkeeper at a small, family-run business. The owner appreciated her work ethic and ability to handle many of the day-to-day crises that popped up in a small business. Terri was able to have the flexible work schedule she needed to continue resolving her personal issues, and soon became "one of the family" at her company. It took a lot of work, patience and determination, but this opportunity has given Terri the confidence to return to the workforce and put her on good footing for any future job search.

Failing to Overcome the Barriers

Earl experienced a different process than Terri, that impeded his ability to get a job.

Since he was not ready to consider work that would imply any loss in status, career services were directed toward helping him analyze his transferable skills to identify professional-level jobs for which he could be competitive, and which would place him in a position to use his age as an asset. The next step would be to help him develop strategies for a targeted job search.

With Earl, an employment goal of business analyst, management analyst, or a related title was decided upon based on the transferable skills analysis. The job-seeking strategy was:

1. **Getting a small but meaningful network started.** This included reaching out to at least two former colleagues, telling them about his employment situation and asking for their help in finding jobs *he was targeting*; joining a job search support group; and volunteering at a non-profit agency where he could demonstrate his skills and make new contacts.

2. **Taking a workshop or course on up-to-date financial analysis software.** He needed a major update in this area.

3. **Looking for listings of hidden jobs,** such as on company websites or on smaller, less well known or specialized recruitment sites, or through contacts he made while developing a meaningful network.

4. **Using direct methods of contact** as discussed in Chapter 13.

5. **Using LinkedIn** to find a recruiter who might be willing to work with him.

6. **Targeting companies that are known to seek and hire older workers,** such as through AARP (https://tinyurl.com/ycab67cy).

7. As with Terri, **working on image** through dressing more youthfully. This was a significant issue for Earl.

8. **Re-writing his resume** to reflect the "new" Earl.

So, with Earl, by taking courses, getting new credentials, volunteering, working part-time, and otherwise building credentials, as well as maintaining a positive attitude about learning new things, he would take a big step toward counteracting any employer age bias. Then, presenting his image as a "youthful" skilled achiever, contributor, and learner in his resume and interviews would complete the task.

Unfortunately, Earl was not willing to make even the simplest of these changes. This is not an unusual scenario. In some cases, even making small changes is too much and goes back to many of the issues involving change discussed in Part 2, "The Paradox of Career Change." This is not an indictment of the seriousness of intent about getting a job. It just reflects the reality of whether getting a job or moving on to the next phase of life, in this case retirement, is most feasible. This may be an issue to discuss with family, and if necessary, with a mental health professional. It was certainly an issue for Earl to consider, and in fact, planning for retirement was what he decided to do.

So, age does matter, but its impact can depend on other factors. Age can certainly be a barrier to employment, due to real or imagined employer perceptions; or due to life complicating circumstances, such as illness, disability, or personal circumstances. However, many common barriers can be overcome by how you prepare for and conduct your job search, and how you present yourself, which can transform age from a liability to an asset.

PART 5

Focusing on Limited Change

I have found that mid- or late-career clients who initially show interest in changing careers often opt for either staying put or making minimal changes. As already discussed, big changes can be upending personally and financially, and the results are unknown. So, after some serious exploration, reality often sets in. Even small changes can be difficult, but the risks are usually lower. After exploring the options, it often seems more practical to take the minimal change route.

Part 5 addresses minimal change strategies that offer ways of addressing common problems that for many of us take the joy out of work. When successfully applied, the results of these efforts can restore or renew a sense of lost work passion and meaning.

CHAPTER 18

In-House Career Development

Photo by Rawpixel

I frequently speak to people in mid-career who express boredom with their jobs or discomfort about where their career is going. Among the nagging thoughts in the forefront are: "Is it time to change my career?" or "Should I look for a new job somewhere else?" This kind of thinking often comes from high achievers who have reached the limits of promotional opportunity, but who have creative or productive capacity that's not being used.

Sometimes these issues legitimately need to be addressed by nothing less than a career or job change. However, in many cases the dissatisfaction can be resolved with little or none of the life disruption that such major change would entail.

This chapter addresses simple, but often ignored, limited career-change strategies to restore or enhance passion and meaning in your work. It builds on earlier discussion and examples in the book about change possibilities within your current work setting; changes *you* can initiate.

For those who work in an organization which is a good fit, it can be productive to explore internal options. That's not always easy though, because of concerns about how it may look if you express what could be dissatisfaction. So, approaching a supervisor, team leader, practice partner, or the human resources department about a change often doesn't seem like a productive option. But maybe it can be.

Talking with a Supervisor

Brenda, a 54-year-old software engineer, works on a development team for an auto manufacturer. She's been with the company in the same job for the past seven years and makes a salary in the top 25% of her profession. At this point she's bored and has been for the past year and a half. She's a reliable, high-quality worker, but rarely gets much day-to-day feedback about her work.

Performance evaluations are done formally on a yearly basis by the department manager, who gets feedback from Brenda's team leader. Her evaluations have been good and accompanied by bonuses for three of the past five years. However, there is rarely what she would call meaningful career development discussion as a part of these meetings or at any other time. Brenda doesn't talk about her boredom to her team members or to the team leader, mainly because she doesn't want to be viewed as a "whiner" and possibly jeopardize her future ability to get bonuses.

In some organizations, supervisor-employee career discussions are a routine part of regular meetings and performance evaluations. However, as in Brenda's case, the culture sometimes doesn't emphasize that. In such places, busy supervisors often overlook the career development function in evaluation meetings or in everyday discussions. When it is addressed, the discussion is short and superficial.

For employees, this can lead to chronic uncertainty regarding one's career and future with the organization, as well as little or no opportunity for renewal. So, getting this process to happen may require a proactive stance.

If you are viewed as valuable to the organization and you have a positive relationship with your supervisor, discussing development concerns can be a productive experience. It can open up new possibilities and alert a supervisor that more attention needs to be paid to keeping the work meaningful and fulfilling. After all, if you are a strong asset, it's in the supervisor's and organization's best interests to retain you as an employee while assuring you maintain passion for your work. Such discussions can also build more productive relationships because a new level of trust is established.

Brenda already has a trusting relationship with both her team leader and the department manager. Still, she is the only woman on her team, and feels that her gender in combination with looking like she is complaining would create a stereotypical view of "female behavior" in this traditional, all-male group.

If you decide to open a career development discussion with your supervisor, how you approach and frame the discussion is important. It need not be structured as a complaint session, but rather one in which you are requesting help with how you can best develop further within the organization. Use the discussion to show how your development would contribute positively to the team, as well as to the supervisor's career and goals for the organization.

For example, if you want to increase challenge and opportunity for advancement, you might ask if you can be assigned to lead a project you know is important to the supervisor; that is, one that if done well would increase his standing in the organization. Thus, if he trusts you to do it and you do well, everyone's advancement potential and positive visibility will increase.

In Brenda's case, she thought developing skills in a newly emerging programming language could help the team develop advanced software that would improve the accuracy of electrical system troubleshooting. She would get the training, train other team members, and then play a leadership role in team development of the new software. She prepared well and set up an appointment to talk with her team leader about the idea. She essentially wanted the company to pay for the training, and for her to be assigned some lead development responsibilities. The costs to the company would be about $8,000 for Brenda's training plus time expended to get other team members trained.

Brenda wanted to speak to the department manager about it, but first wanted support of the team leader. He agreed that this would be a good project for the team, for him (if Brenda's plan worked), and for the company. Thus, he decided to make the presentation to the department head himself, with Brenda present.

What happened here is that instead of complaining about her boredom, Brenda converted her problem into a career development project that would create a new training experience, potential to provide leadership on a new project, and a chance to create a breakthrough for the company that would make everyone in the department look good. That would certainly ameliorate her boredom!

Team Interventions—Marty's Plan

Sometimes a group of team members can initiate a grassroots effort to infuse new energy where boredom and stagnation are setting in. To do this without sending the wrong message to managers, it's necessary to be in a culture of open communication; have trusting, positive relationships with management; and be ready to lead a group of individuals who have similar concerns and feelings.

Photo by Geralt

Jensen-Jones Group is a small health care consulting firm. It's a flat organization with no middle managers. There are fourteen health care consultants and five partners currently handling five service lines at a variety of hospitals and other health organizations on the east coast. Jensen-Jones hires and retains top tier consultants who are experts in their fields and well-respected nationally.

Several of these mid-career employees have been with the company for ten or more years, and although they make very good salaries and receive regular bonuses, there is little or no opportunity for advancement to partner. With little chance of career progression and a sense of boredom setting in, these employees feel stuck in their careers. However, they fit well with the company, are comfortable with their salaries and benefits, and most have stable family situations that they don't want to upend by changing jobs.

In response to this situation, one of the consultants, Marty, decided to initiate an ad hoc work group to study the problem. Informal leaders from the different service lines met during off-work hours and decided to create a plan to present to the partners. The plan would both develop sales opportunities across service lines and build mechanisms to develop younger associates. The partners were informed that the group would be meeting about this and were supportive of what the group was trying to achieve.

The idea would be to reinforce and support a growth component of the company culture, as well as increase company financial performance. For Marty, just planning and organizing this effort was an energizing project. Leading the group to develop a viable plan and get management support would potentially create longer-term development opportunities and the satisfaction and recognition of helping the company become more successful.

Unintended and Other Opportunities
For Brenda, it turned out that the department manager chose to defer pursuing her plan because of other company priorities and some budget restraints. However, he was genuinely grateful to her for the effort she put into her proposal. This led to an in-depth discussion about her career with the company.

In this context, she could express her concerns about boredom without feeling she was jeopardizing her position or her career. She and the department manager were able to agree on a plan that would have her working in her original job part of the time. The manager arranged with another department to share her time consulting with a team of mechanical engineers who needed software engineering services.

This arrangement enhanced her reputation more broadly within the company and reflected positively on her team leader and the department manager. Most importantly, she was now entering a job situation that was newly challenging and offered genuine opportunities for future promotion.

As with Brenda, changes within your work unit may not always work out as intended, or with the otherwise positive end results she had. However, if you fit well in a large enough organization, there may be other opportunities.

It may be necessary to do some internal job searching. Depending upon how communications take place, this could be a sensitive and sometimes long-term process. If the structure is loose, with communications taking place at all levels, you can be exploring the possibilities for opportunities all the time while using your informal, internal company network. If communications are chain-of-command oriented, it may be more appropriate to make your interests known to the human resources department or respond to formal job announcements.

In either case, if possible, communication about your interest in changing jobs should occur with your supervisor or team leader as part of a career development discussion. Otherwise, you face the possibility of anger, resentment, loss of trust, or even attempts to sabotage what you are trying to do. The organization culture and rules usually dictate formally and informally how one should go about moving to different jobs internally.

At Jensen-Jones Group, Marty's plan also didn't work out exactly as hoped. It was presented to a few of the partners. They were pleased with the effort because the ad hoc team had already developed momentum. That precluded the need for the partners to do any of the work. However, the plan didn't develop any steam, mainly because the partners were focused mostly on getting and keeping business. Employee development was not a priority or of much interest. It was judged that none of the consultants were likely to leave the company. They were well paid, had good benefits, and had enough challenging work to do. Thus, the need to take energy or resources away from the core mission was simply not there at the time the plan was presented.

However, some positives for the consultants came from the effort. It made the partners more aware of consultant concerns about professional development. Subsequently, consultants were invited to join new leadership activities and committees. In addition, working on the project strengthened connections among consultant colleagues.

For Marty, all this had at least a temporary effect on his positive feelings about his work and his contribution to his colleagues, as well as the organization. With continued participation in leadership activities and decisions, the greater sense of involvement may have a longer-term motivating effect, alleviate some of the boredom, and among consultants, provide a sense that upward mobility within the company is still possible.

Taking the soft approach of exploring within the organization can sometimes bring a renewed sense of passion and meaning in your work, and save the costs, uncertainty, and emotional stress of a major career shake-up. At the very least, even a slight change can revitalize things for a while or have positive long-term consequences. If this doesn't work, you can still consider the next step of changing your career or finding a job in a different place.

CHAPTER 19

Working with an Unbearable Supervisor

What Toll is it Taking?

When I hear someone say, "I'd like to kill that woman (or man)," referring to a supervisor, I quickly take notice and ask, "What do you mean?" Usually it's just a way of venting extreme frustration and not anywhere near a serious statement of intent. I suspect many more employees fantasize in those terms than say it, but no one except the most mentally unstable would try to solve such problems through physical violence.

If you're having serious, chronic difficulty with a supervisor, it can be mind boggling and stressful beyond belief. Anger, fear, frustration, chronic anxiety, illness, self-doubt, loss of self-worth, and loss of interest in your job or career run rampant. It can affect every aspect of your life and result in an acute or chronic stagnating work situation.

Before starting my own company, I had a lengthy career with some truly great mentors and supervisors along the way. However, I also had some supervisors with whom I could not relate, who were non-supportive, or who were downright hostile to me and impeded my advancement. These were some very frustrating periods. Now, when I hear clients talk about anger and frustration with supervisors, I always think of how incredibly difficult this can be.

If it's happening or has happened to you, you know that it's just about impossible to maintain any degree of passion for or meaning in the work you are doing. You're more likely to be focusing on getting rebuffed, being ignored or treated disrespectfully, feeling extreme discomfort, or even wondering, "When am I going to get fired?"

Allison's Harassment

Allison is a married 32-year-old sideline reporter for a major league baseball team. She has a background in print journalism, specifically sports writing, but five years ago she took an opportunity that was offered by a local baseball franchise to learn broadcasting. She progressed rapidly to her current position, and with her high TV ratings, has the potential to move into national broadcasting. She loves her work and the lure of fame and fortune, but she has also been considering a change back to writing and expanding into news areas beyond sports. Her situation with her supervisor, the program director has progressed to unbearable. He is on a fast career track and has high esteem among colleagues throughout the baseball world. However, he has made sexual advances to Allison over the past six months, which she has rebuffed. There is gossip about a relationship between them, which is untrue, although it is evident to other employees that he has shown favoritism toward her. At the same time, he has increased her assignments to unworkable levels, which she thinks may be associated with her rebuffing his advances.

His reputation is stellar, and he is not known to be a womanizer, so if she raises the issue with team management it would be her word against his.

As a public figure Allison believes an allegation of sexual harassment against her supervisor could seriously hurt his career and her own. She sees herself in an untenable position that she can no longer tolerate. She can't sleep at night and her relationship with her husband and family is deteriorating. She doesn't know what to do.

Josh Is Furious

Josh is 52 and a nurse case manager for a national health insurance provider. After 30 years as a general duty nurse in military and civilian hospitals, for the past three years he has done home visits and routine phone follow-ups with patients who have chronic medical conditions. He is very dissatisfied with his job mainly because of the relationship with his supervisor. He is furious with the way he has been treated. He left hospital nursing because the work was too heavy, and shifts kept changing. He felt worn out physically and mentally. He expected case management to be less taxing. It is, except that his supervisor keeps criticizing his work and asking him to do follow-up calls to patients to correct deficiencies. Although much of the work is from home, he thinks what he is being asked to do is insulting and unfair. Also, with the time spent on correcting deficiencies he can't meet company productivity requirements without working 50–60 hours per week.

The supervisor is known to be difficult and detail oriented, and he does tend to make employees angry. He has only 10 years of nursing experience but is on an upward career track and is likely to be promoted in the next two years. Josh sees himself as an experienced, competent nurse and doesn't appreciate being treated in a demeaning way. He views this as a good job except for the supervisor. When asked about his situation he says, "I could just murder that guy." He doesn't mean that literally, but it illustrates his rage at the situation.

Why is it Happening?

When considering treatment by a supervisor, the most important question is, what is your role in the problem? Is everyone having issues with this supervisor, or is it mainly you? It's not unusual for people to complain, but some supervisors can be effective in their role, even though they don't get along well with all their employees. So, it's important, even with an unpopular supervisor, to look at what he or she is expecting and whether you can meet those expectations. Was Josh looking inward at whether some of his supervisor's criticisms were reasonable?

Sometimes feedback is limited or non-existent, which makes it more difficult to interpret what your supervisor wants. When the problem is viewed as performance- or conduct-related by the supervisor, and you are not responding as he or she wants, the situation can get worse. You may get poor performance reviews, warning notices, or worse, insidious attempts to get you to leave, also known as the "boil the frog" strategy . . . in other words, making things progressively more difficult until you terminate your own employment, thereby helping the employer avoid legal or other issues that formal termination might bring. Could Josh be the "frog" in this situation?

As things worsen, anger can increase, and passive-aggressive behaviors can occur on both sides, making positive changes almost impossible. So, the point is, if you can identify your role in the problem and make quick changes before things get out of control, that's usually the best strategy. If the problem is simply incompatibility, or if there is a more general problem with this supervisor, other strategies need consideration.

Turning Things Around

So, what can you do about incompatibility with your supervisor, or a supervisor who is difficult for many employees to work with? You're not likely to get your supervisor to change her style or approach too much, nor are you likely to influence the organization to fire him. It happens, but don't depend on it.

Supervisors usually are in sync with their manager's instructions and organization policy, and some are reflecting what they think their managers are asking them to do regardless of how they treat their employees. This was probably the case with Josh. Exceptions might be if you are being asked to perform clearly illegal actions of which higher-level managers are otherwise unaware, or if you are being sexually harassed or otherwise being discriminated against for reasons protected under the law and/or organization policy. Allison thought she might be functioning under these conditions.

Here are some alternatives to consider:

1. **Improve your relationship.** This may be difficult if there's bad blood, especially if you believe you are being treated unfairly, inconsistently or are in a hostile environment. It may be impossible if you are experiencing sexual harassment, illegal discrimination, or you are being asked to do things you believe are wrong, illegal, or unethical. If the relationship seems salvageable, it may take strong efforts on your part and swallowing your pride, but compromises can be achieved with a supervisor or an organization that views you as valuable. If you talk about the issues and still can't make progress or the handwriting on the wall says you're on your way out, you're probably in a no-win situation. Was discussing the problems a reasonable alternative for Allison or Josh? Could Allison use common knowledge about the #metoo movement to subly influence her supervisor? Certainly he would be concerned about a "trashed" career because of a credible sexual harassment charge.

2. **Request transfer to another unit and apply for jobs in other units.** This can work nicely in large organizations. It's a win-win for a supervisor and for the organization if you're perceived by others in the management chain as high functioning, and the conflict with your supervisor is simply seen as a personality conflict. This was an alternative that worked well for Sammy the Sensitive in chapter 6.

3. **Go through grievance or legal procedures.** If you belong to a union, or the organization has grievance procedures in place, you can go this route. Unions can provide support, help in managing anger, and possibly influence management. If you believe you are being harassed or discriminated against illegally and have exhausted organization and union options, you can file complaints with the proper government entity. Finally, you can consider a lawsuit. However, with any of these options, be prepared for long, drawn-out adversarial activities which may or may not solve the underlying issues, may cause protracted aggravation and stress, may set up ongoing adversary work relationships, and may result in a case you could lose. These routes may also not be best if you are hoping for later advancement, particularly if you lose your case. This is a situation Allison was facing if she decided to go in one of these directions.

4. **Build your life away from your current job.** If you get your strongest satisfactions from work activities, consider slowly starting a small business in your off-work hours, such as consulting, privately providing your professional services, an internet sales business or a business related to a hobby. If the business builds, you can decide whether you want to do it full-time. For some people, a new, more satisfying career has roots in dissatisfaction with a prior job. If you do not see work as central to your life, consider further developing your hobbies, family involvements, social activities, and friendships. Engaging in volunteer work can also provide personally satisfying and meaningful experiences. Finally, taking courses and workshops either work related or not can build new skills and bring focus to other areas of interest.

5. **Wait for the supervisor to leave.** On occasion, it may be worthwhile to just be patient and wait it out. Some managers are on the fast track to promotion or retirement and will be gone quickly. In both Allison's and Josh's case, their supervisors were likely to be promoted within the next few years.

6. **Look elsewhere for a new job.** This may be the best alternative if you can't improve the relationship, cannot find another job within the organization, or are in a period of performance improvement and are not showing progress. This may also be the most constructive exit if you are considering, but do not have tolerance for, the stresses of protracted adversarial procedures that may not end in your favor. In other words, cut your losses before things get worse. Would this be something Allison should consider?

Dealing with difficult supervisory relationships is exasperating and usually complex. Unless your supervisor is likely to leave soon, it may be to the benefit of your health and well-being to quickly resolve the issues or move on. On the other hand, if your emotions reach a point where you are under excessive stress, or you believe you could lose control and do harm, seek support from a mental health professional as soon as possible. Easily accessible mental health resources are discussed in chapter 30.

CHAPTER 20

Feeling Unappreciated

Photo by ID 33489558 © Hongqi Zhang (aka Michael Zhang) | Dreamstime.com

Nobody Really Cares

Over my career, I don't know how many times I've heard expressions like "they just don't appreciate what I do" or "no one acknowledges how important we are to this organization", but it's been a lot!

You may recognize these words because you feel this way yourself and feeling degraded makes you angry and frustrated. If it's chronic, you may be complaining a lot or looking to go elsewhere. So, what does this mean? Feeling unappreciated at work feeds a perception that who you are and what you do is not acknowledged as being important. In reality, you may be appreciated but not know it, or you may know you're appreciated but don't think you're appreciated enough—or you may be correct in the sense that you aren't appreciated at all!

Let's examine some reasons you may feel unappreciated at work and what you can do rather than remaining frustrated or moving on to a change in job or career.

Non-Critical Work

The work you do may not be as critical as you think. That is, you do a great job, but the focus of the organization is on other work.

Dr. Holloway is director of counseling services at a state university. Although applications for mental health counseling have been increasing over the past two years, funding for more staff has decreased. Most other programs at the university have received small to moderate increases. Dr. Holloway sees her program as highly important, since it helps students with serious personal problems, and quite successfully, she believes. So, since the need is there, why is her funding decreasing?

Although she consistently touts the success of her program to university administrators, there are higher priorities. The results of counseling are hard to measure. Most administrators give lip service about the importance of counseling services, yet they are not willing to commit funding over instructional and research programs which are mission-centered and bring funds into the university. This has been an ongoing problem with this low-profile counseling services program. So, there is a discrepancy between Dr. Holloway's perception of her program's high importance vs. what decision-makers at the university treat as a non-critical program. To Dr. Holloway and her staff counselors, this feels a lot like a total lack of appreciation for the good work they do.

In situations like these, where the work is not viewed as an organizational priority, most feelings of appreciation need to come from recognition by peers, clients, and possibly from a supervisor. Peer recognition can come from staff assuming leadership roles in professional organizations, giving presentations, teaching, workshops, and writing. For example, Dr. Holloway requested to teach a course in counseling theories in the Counselor Education Department at the university. This gave her the opportunity to gain recognition among peers and students in an instructional program.

Getting feedback from clients can also provide concrete expressions of appreciation. In Dr. Holloway's case, she was encouraged by the university provost to develop a formal system to measure and report on client satisfaction to university administrators. While this would be useful to the university in assessing value and funding needs, it would also serve as a vehicle for Dr. Holloway and the counselors to get concrete feedback about their work and to improve services. Positive satisfaction results would also reinforce how students benefit and the gratitude they feel toward the counselors.

Dr. Holloway purchased a client satisfaction measurement system, and in the first round of surveys it was found that students were very positive and satisfied. The surveys showed that counseling services were a major factor in users remaining at the university rather than dropping out. When seeing the results, Dr. Holloway's supervisor, the dean of student affairs, was effusive in his praise of the program to incoming students during the next freshman orientation. He also authorized small monetary bonuses and certificates of achievement to all program staff. All of this was a great boost to Dr. Holloway's and the counselors' feelings about themselves and about the value of the counseling program. For the first time they felt appreciated for the importance of their work. Funding for two new counselors was also later approved in the next fiscal year budget.

What Does She Actually Do?

In some instances, managers or leaders may not understand what you do. This is most likely when you are in a specialized support role or when the type or complexity of the work you do is unfamiliar to others. For example, if your job focuses on social network marketing or public relations, it may be difficult for others to know exactly what you do with your time. You talk to a lot of people and are at your computer, but the work you do doesn't concretely translate to bottom-line results, like increased sales or customer satisfaction. The connection may be there, but it's indirect and not readily apparent or measurable.

So, what do you do? In this case, educating the right people is important. The key to effective educating is relationship-building *with those who can benefit from communication about what you do*; then keeping what you do and the results you see *regularly on the front burner.*

Xavier, the director of social network marketing at a large non-profit social services agency, was having a difficult time explaining what he did with his time. In fact, he heard from a Board member that the agency was considering reducing his job to half-time. To preserve his full-time status, he found that he had to request a meeting bi-weekly with the CEO to keep her informed about what he was posting on social media sites about the agency, what the CEO wanted to be publicized, what results the CEO wanted to see from each effort, and whether the desired results were being achieved. In that way, the social media initiatives were not just another program buried in the mix of programs supporting the direct service mission of the agency. Social media marketing became an approach the CEO began to see as a priority that was benefiting the agency's financial bottom line and prestige within the community.

> **You may think you're working hard, or harder than anyone else and doing a better job, but if others don't, or don't at least acknowledge your value to each other, your work won't get appreciation.**

How Others Perceive You

The perception by others about how well you do your job or your contribution to the team effort may be different than yours. When it comes to receiving appreciation, it's the external observers that count: managers, co-workers, colleagues, customers, boards of directors, stockholders, and sometimes, the public. You may think you're working hard, or harder than anyone else and doing a better job, but if others don't, or don't at least acknowledge your value to each other, your work won't get appreciation.

Worse yet is others perceiving you as a complainer, or problem creator rather than a problem-solver. This definitely will not engender appreciation . . . rather just the opposite. Sometimes personality conflicts, team competition, or politics may influence how you are perceived. Be careful about dismissing the possibility that your performance or attitude could be better, or that you could improve as a team contributor. Negative perceptions of this nature often take a long time to change, so expect peer and manager responses to your efforts at change to be slow. This situation also carries the risk of alienation or job loss. If you sense that the team or organization is giving up on you, it may be worth getting a fresh start somewhere else before being forced out or enduring the "torture" of staying.

Photo by ID 97318901 © Halifah Rahmansyah | Dreamstime.com

Perceptions are often difficult to accurately assess. Before Dr. Holloway did studies of her program's effectiveness, she would always get good feedback from administrators when she asked how they viewed the counseling program. They knew she wanted to hear good things and no one wanted to risk unnecessary conflicts with her. Unfortunately, this was not the same discussion that took place in budget meetings or private meetings among administrators. In fact, there was heavy competition for limited funds and some decision makers thought the counseling program could be cut back in scope. This led to the decrease in Dr. Holloway's allocation.

Non-Rewarding Culture

You may work for a manager or organization that doesn't nurture or reward positives. For example, in some places the underlying approach is "management by exception." That is, you get feedback mainly when you do something wrong, or that's what you remember most. If the culture, or a supervisor who doesn't frequently recognize or reward, is the problem, then it may be necessary to *ask* for feedback, particularly when you think you've done well on something. Some managers and supervisors are slower to give unsolicited praise than others, and some rarely do. You might interpret that as meaning you are doing a mediocre job and unappreciated. *Asking for feedback* can have a positive effect if you are seen as doing excellent work but rarely informed of it.

Underpaid and Under-promoted

With all you do, you may feel underpaid or under-promoted. Although many people feel under paid, the question is whether you really are. Base salary can represent the norm for your occupation. That may be low compared to how you see the value of what you do, e.g., school teachers. Or you may be paid according to company pay schedules and policy. This isn't an appreciation issue, unless you are paid less than those standards dictate. You have the choice to look for a higher-paying job or prepare for a higher-paying occupation.

Pay changes, like a bonus, salary increase, or promotion, usually represent appreciation. If you don't make partner in the firm and a colleague does, you'll feel underappreciated if you know or believe your contribution was better. Relationship-building with supervisors, openly discussing concerns, and understanding compensation rules are important in dealing with these issues. In some instances, if the facts confirm chronic unfair treatment, it may be best to follow appeal procedures, take legal steps to correct the inequity, or look for a job elsewhere.

I Get No Respect . . . Anywhere

If you feel unappreciated in most areas of your personal life, with your spouse, family, friends, and in non-work activities, you may be feeling a general sense of unhappiness. This is likely to carry over to your feelings about appreciation at work. Unhappiness or depression can have a blunting effect on all positive things that happen. So even when appreciation is expressed for your work, you may not notice, or downplay it. If this is happening it may be worthwhile to seek professional counseling to help improve your overall life satisfaction. This is discussed further in chapter 29.

Chances are that feelings about lack of appreciation are due to some combination of the above factors. However, as illustrated by the 80/20 rule in chapter 5, sometimes even minor changes can have a broad impact on all the causes. In fact, research (https://tinyurl.com/ybhz3dfe) suggests that something as simple as expressing appreciation and gratitude more to others increases well-being, happiness, relationships, optimism, and improves physical and mental health.[14] Giving appreciation may in fact be an antidote for feelings of not being appreciated!

---

[14] PPP Editorial Team (2017). What is Gratitude and What is Its Role in Positive Psychology, Positive Psychology Program, (https://positivepsychologyprogram.com/gratitude-appreciation/#effects)

PART 6

Managing the Emotions of a Difficult Job Search

When a job search is unproductive, it takes a toll. Depression, anxiety, and the urge to give up can take over your life. Discouragement is a normal response. But if this goes on for a prolonged period, you can dig deeper and deeper into a hole. It may affect all aspects of your life, including the success of your ability to find the right job, or even any job.

Chapters 21 and 22 address reversing and coping with discouragement and depression, the most common emotional symptoms associated with a long and difficult job search.

CHAPTER 21

Discouragement and Depression During a Long Job Search

Photo by Geralt

Feeling the Pain

If you've ever looked for a job for a long time, I don't need to tell you about discouragement. And maybe I don't need to tell you about depression, the next step.

You already know how difficult it is to face another day of failure or rejection, feeling like a failure as a family provider, or inadequacy as a spouse/partner. If you are without spouse or partner, or a single parent or provider for a family, you likely are worried about how long you can last with little or no income coming in.

You may have already read articles or talked to others who tell you that it's normal to feel discouraged, so you don't feel abnormal. Unfortunately, discouragement begins to affect your whole life, including your effectiveness in job searching, the issue that got you to this point in the first place. If you continue to be discouraged or if you already have a propensity toward emotional lows, discouragement may gradually turn to depression, or worsen existing depression.

Symptoms of depression are more pervasive than discouragement, and if something new for you, depression represents an emotional change from how you were before. You may feel sad and have lost interest or pleasure in the normal activities of your life. Over time, depression symptoms have impact on some combination of mood, appetite, sleep, energy, self-esteem, concentration, decision-making, and feelings of hopelessness. Depression can be mild, or it can be a severe but highly treatable medical condition.

In my experience of dealing with long-term job seekers, whether discouraged or depressed, it's very difficult to mobilize energy to deal with the situation. That's why this can feed on itself and worsen. So how can you cope and prevent or deal with a downhill slide while continuing a productive search?

High-Impact Methods of Coping with Discouragement

When discouragement is the major issue, finding an excellent job is the ultimate cure. So, the obvious action is to improve your job search strategy or change your job target. If you've already done those things, you're on the right track. If you haven't, chapter 22 addresses focusing on a detailed reexamination of the essential steps in your job search method.

However, if you're following a sound strategy and still haven't found a job, coping with discouragement is best done with a formal social support system. Try to find a job search support group in your community. My experience as a group facilitator is that support from people in similar situations can have an amazing effect. I have seen people try job-search techniques successfully that they never would have done on their own, members who decide on a new, unexpected path, and others who, just by attending a session or two, have a new perspective on their job search.

Marcy, an unemployed travel agent, heard about our group of job seekers and decided to attend. She came to one weekly meeting, then had to miss the next three weeks due to out-of-town commitments. She never returned. However, I found out from another group member that she got a new job. A month or so later she saw me at a street fair and came over to talk. She told me how the group helped her to feel revived and motivated her to keep on with her job search.

She credited the group experience for her success in finding a new job. Personally, it was hard to figure out what she was talking about: that kind of impact after one session? However, I believe she was genuinely expressing her response to the group experience, and the power of even a taste of social support, knowing that she was not alone and that group members were supporting her efforts.

The remarkable thing about job-search support groups is that you are meeting with people who are experiencing feelings very like your own. You can't imagine the power of that until you experience it. Often the composition of such groups can be quite diverse. You might be surprised to see a CEO who lost her job, a laid-off manager and clerical worker, an attorney looking for a new job, and an auto mechanic wanting to change occupations, all in the same group. Despite this diversity, feelings and ideas shared and the mutual help provided can have the immediate impact of reducing the sense of loneliness that comes with discouragement.

If you've been reticent about finding a support group, don't let your discouragement stop you. Look for groups at non-profit agencies that offer career services, a local careeronestop center, the library, or a local community college.

You may be able to benefit further by using stress-reduction techniques, such as muscle relaxation (https://tinyurl.com/ztn6rom), deep breathing (https://tinyurl.com/4s5oq2), and mindfulness meditation (https://tinyurl.com/pnms66r). This will help you avoid letting anxiety about job seeking and rejection impact negatively on how you are going through the process. The links provided are sources for basic professional advice on how to regularly practice these activities. More advanced assistance can be found through consulting with a mental health professional.

Another simple coping strategy is to consider a regular exercise program. Research shows that exercise tends to enhance emotional well-being. This won't solve your job-search problems, but it can be helpful in counteracting the negative emotions associated with both discouragement and depression. If you have medical problems and are just beginning, be sure to check with your health care professional to assure that you start at a safe level without injury.

Coping with Depression

If you have significant depression, you will likely be experiencing symptoms beyond discouragement over an extended period. The symptoms may be worsening and affecting most aspects of your life. Others may observe that you are not the same person you once were, and you may feel that your self-esteem is at an all-time low.

While discouragement is inevitable during a long job search, it is important to use early or pre-emptive coping strategies to avoid or counteract a downward spiral toward depression or exacerbation of already existing depression.

If depression is in the early stages, mild, and clearly an extension of discouragement with your career situation, then it is all the more important to seek the social support discussed above. If you cannot muster the energy or enthusiasm to do this, then it's time to see a mental health professional. Licensed mental health counselors, professional counselors, psychologists, social workers, and psychiatric nurses, are trained to help you get back your emotional equilibrium, so you can move on with your life.

If you are feeling hopeless and having thoughts of suicide, it is most important that you promptly consult with a licensed mental health professional, particularly a psychiatrist, if one is available. You can get a referral from your family doctor or do an internet search for a local community mental health center or a family service agency in your area. In most places in the U.S., you can also dial 211 to speak to someone who can refer you to a local community service.

If you are at the point of seriously contemplating suicide, please call the National Suicide Prevention Hotline (1-800-273-TALK). A trained suicide prevention worker will listen and help you. Finally, if suicide action is imminent, go to a hospital emergency department to get immediate medical treatment, or if too distressed to do that, call 911.

Pre-Empt Serious Trouble

While discouragement is inevitable during a long job search, it is important to use early or pre-emptive coping strategies to avoid or counteract a downward spiral toward depression or exacerbation of already existing depression. Obviously this is difficult, because to keep from falling deeper, your actions need to run counter to what you are feeling. Try to be aware of what you are dealing with early and the options you can exercise in getting yourself back on track to effectively work toward an emotional balance and a more positive job search experience.

CHAPTER 22

Strategies to Reverse Discouragement and Depression

Photo by PhotografielLink

Taking a Fresh Look

Chapter 21 addressed coping with discouragement and depression. This chapter goes a step further and considers substantive actions you can take to reverse the negative emotions surrounding a long and discouraging job search. In fact, some of the strategies, if followed, may change your direction entirely and begin to provide a renewed sense of life purpose.

You may already be doing some of these things, but the difference here is in intensity and commitment to change in your daily life. The idea is to fill your time with activity that improves effectiveness of your job search; brings in some income while you are searching; makes you feel positive about yourself, and your contributions to others; and facilitates getting your career back on track.

Strategy 1—Reexamine Your Job-Search Method

If you are intent on continuing to look for full-time employment in the same field you left, it will be productive to do a re-examination of your job search methodology to include:

- Job goal
- Resume building
- How you are reaching employers
- Interviewing presentation and strategies
- Interview follow-up activities
- Negotiation strategy
- Deal-closing

The re-examination is an intensive process requiring a lot of time on your part and, in fact, may even lead to changing careers. Parts 3 and 4 of this book will help you through the process.

Although you can do this re-examination on your own, you can also enlist the help of a career guidance or job placement professional as your partner in the process. You can find help through listings published by the National Career Development Association (https://tinyurl.com/yd5qwelc), or consider free services of the American Job Centers (https://tinyurl.com/y7mzprs2).

Strategy 2—Get a Part-Time Job

Do part-time paid work, and if you can, locate something in your field or one closely related. I have had clients who've done such jobs as substitute teaching in public schools, Uber and Lyft driving, teaching courses as adjunct college instructors, and seasonal tax preparation, while searching for a full-time job.

If you can't find something in your field, try something else that may use your skills. In fact, some find that stringing together several part-time jobs provides the flexibility and variety for a more enjoyable and lucrative option than full-time employment. See chapter 28 to get some specific suggestions for part-time employment, including professional consulting opportunities. That chapter addresses retirement options, but the jobs suggested can apply to anyone looking for part-time work that uses prior skills. Legitimate part-time opportunities for home-based employment can also be found at Human Services Outcomes, Inc (https://tinyurl.com/y9xk3cb4).

Strategy 3—Volunteer

Until you have enough paid work, do part-time volunteer work that you consider important. This will keep you involved in activities that are meaningful to you and to others. That will contribute to improved mood, and feelings of self-worth. You may also make contacts with people who can help with getting a full-time job or other part-time work. Volunteering can also add to your list of current references and show potential future employers that you are remaining fully active. Visit Volunteer Match (http://www.volunteermatch.org/) to find meaningful volunteer work in your community.

Strategy 4—Start a Small Business

Under some circumstances, starting a business can be an energizing process. I say this with extreme caution, because as a full-time venture this is a risky strategy. Per U.S. government data, around 50% of new businesses fail within about five years (https://tinyurl.com/y7356mh7). Some, such as construction and retail, appear to have higher failure rates than others (https://tinyurl.com/ya8qah5f). However, starting a business can be a great alternative if:

- You have a skill or product that is in demand and can be sold
- You have the patience to develop the business skills required to start and run a business
- You are willing to spend very long days during start-up and beyond
- You want to try developing a part-time business that you can sustain even after you find a traditional job. This can work if you have a product to sell, or a service to provide, such as personal training, physical therapy, website development, or teaching music. If the business takes off, you can look to doing it full-time. If the business cannot provide an adequate income, you can consider other part-time work to equal a total of full-time work, or you can opt for a full-time job when you find one, while also maintaining the part-time business. Developing a business can be a motivating diversion while you look for a traditional job. However, the risk is that

you split your time and cannot focus your energy enough in either direction.

I can tell you from my own and others' experiences, when you are starting a business you believe in, you can get giddy with enthusiasm, forget your prior discouragement, and do not have time to look back! In your own business, you can have a full sense of control of your destiny. This can be an exhilarating experience and a new lease on your career, particularly if you left or lost a job in which you were dissatisfied, were often engaged in conflict, experienced the humiliation of a termination or layoff, or if you are transitioning out of military service.

However, a good idea alone for a business won't work. You must be able to develop (or already have) the skills to start up and manage the business. You must take responsibility for the business vision, leadership, customer service, marketing, and a multitude of business management issues from the financial to the legal. Fortunately, there are plenty of resources available to help, starting with SCORE (http://www.score.org/), the Small Business Administration (https://tinyurl.com/zmk29wm), and local community economic development programs offering free workshops and consultation.

Fighting Against the Paradox of Reversing Discouragement

As you can see, the underlying theme of the four strategies is to counteract discouragement through full engagement in personally meaningful activities. These should keep you socially connected and support resuming the same or even a new career as soon as possible.

However, if you are feeling discouraged or are depressed, restructuring your life around a new, intensive mix of activities may be challenging. After all, the worse you feel, the more difficult it is to focus and make changes, let alone big changes.

The worse you feel, the more difficult it is to focus and make changes, let alone big changes.

If you find this to be true, start slowly with a volunteer activity, or join a job search support group, and start an exercise program, as discussed in chapter 21, as a coping strategy. As your self-esteem improves, you will feel like moving forward on a more intensive basis. If you find starting this too difficult or you struggle with ongoing depression, then engagement with a mental health professional will get the ball rolling in the right direction.

PART 7

Managing Work and Disability

By mid-career and into our late 50s, 60s, 70s and beyond, physical illness and disability[15] *increasingly play a role in the type of work we can do and to what extent we can work, if at all. Mental illnesses, including alcohol and drug use and abuse, also impact the ability to perform a job at all career stages. Most mid- and late-career clients I have worked with, not initially presenting with an illness or disability, actually do have some condition that they later divulge which impacts on work now, has in the past, or will in the future. The gamut includes physical, mental, and alcohol-related problems.*

Illnesses, such as cancer or heart disease, can appear unexpectedly. Accidents can happen at any time and create life chaos, including financial, health care, and work issues. Some medical conditions create disabilities over time and require a change in job or occupation. In some instances, work needs to be reduced to part-time. In others, work is not feasible at all. These are very serious issues that many of us face. The chapters in Part 7 deal with the realities and solutions.

In this book, the focus is on maximizing the ability to do work that elicits a continuing sense of passion and meaning. When financial concerns

---

15   Disability has different meanings for different purposes. For example, per the Americans With Disabilities Act, it is defined as an individual's physical or mental impairment that substantially limits one or more major life activities for that individual. The Social Security definition specifically refers to inability to work. Workers Compensation laws have multiple definitions for disability, and disability insurance policies define disability differently. For purposes of this book, we use the general dictionary definition "a physical, mental, cognitive, or developmental condition that impairs, interferes with, or limits a person's ability to engage in certain tasks or actions or participate in typical daily activities and interactions" (https://www.merriam-webster .com/dictionary/disability).

intervene, which they often will with illness and disability, the idea is still to do as much as is feasible to achieve that goal of passion and meaning for any work that you can do, within the boundaries of your circumstances.

CHAPTER 23

Coping with Medical Limitations, Disability, or Illness

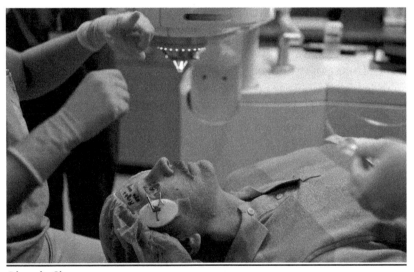

Photo by Skeeze

Juggling Illness or Disability and a Meaningful Career

For many years, I've worked with career issues of people with disabilities. I've testified in thousands of Social Security disability hearings regarding whether people can work, and if so, what they can do. I've also employed individuals with disabilities or medical issues, as well as maneuvered through some of my own.

If you are in a professional career and have medical limitations, disability, or illness impacting your ability to do your job or even be at work, how do you manage? This is a common experience, especially as we age into mid-career and later. However, if you enjoy working, are entrenched in your career, or have financial needs, you probably worry about your future and feel conflicted in what to do.

You don't need to have an overwhelming or even obvious medical issue to be concerned. Medical limitations, disability, and illness come in various forms. When you think of disability, you may automatically think of a person needing a wheelchair, someone who can't use an arm or speak clearly due to a stroke, or someone who is blind. Many more of us have hidden limitations and impairments, resulting from "silent" conditions such as heart disease, cancer, liver disease, HIV, orthopedic injuries, and so forth, which make life more difficult but manageable. However, these conditions can become more functionally limiting and disabling over time.

For those of us entrenched in a career, we find ourselves wanting to continue using our skills and making meaningful contributions, despite our health limitations.

Many of these conditions gradually require more missed work days for treatment, result in a slower work pace and inability to do certain aspects of the job, and they may negatively impact ability to stay focused on the work. No one sees the condition when they look at you, but it's there and affecting you. Eventually, others may see the effects, but may not understand what's happening, or why performance in going downhill.

If you have a "silent" medical condition that impacts on ability to perform your job now, or might in the near future, you may keep your concerns private for fear of jeopardizing your job status, advancement potential, or even insurance benefits. Although the

Americans with Disabilities Act (https://www.ada.gov/) mandates certain employer actions, you may have refrained from playing that card because of unspoken bias, question of its application to your issues, or how it might affect your co-workers.

The Cases of Sandy, Angela, Jose, and Jack

Consider these situations: Sandy is a 49-year-old hospital RN with longstanding back problems. Her work has always required lifting patients and other strenuous activity. She now requires increased medication to manage pain at and off work. She loves being a nurse, but something needs to change.

Angela is a 54-year-old college dean, but more and more her lupus and fibromyalgia are causing missed work, including critical meetings and speaking commitments. She pushes herself but feels like she operates at 60% and is declining.

Jose, a 45-year-old bank branch manager, has had ongoing treatments for lung cancer. He continues to be able to work, but due to missed time and fatigue, he can't keep up with his job duties.

Jack is 47 and a retired Army officer with an information technology background. He served tours in Iraq and Afghanistan before returning home. He started having panic attacks after leaving the service. So far, he's been unable to search for a civilian job because of his fear of leaving his house. He receives compensation payments for his disability from the Department of Veterans Affairs (VA), and a pension from his military retirement. Aside from needing more income to maintain his family's usual living standard, he really wants a meaningful civilian career.

All of these workers are ready for or in need of some change. Sandy pretty much keeps her problems to herself but knows this can't go on much longer. She could ask the hospital to make reasonable accommodations for her under the Americans with Disabilities Act by modifying her workload, but she is uncomfortable making an issue of her disability and she would not want to increase the workload burden on the other nurses. One option would be to find a more sedentary job, such as an advice nurse in a physician's office or with an insurance company. It's not where the action is, but she could continue to use her nursing skills.

Angela is more likely to need a change in career path that allows flexibility to work fewer hours and on her own schedule. Her medical situation is known to the college, as is her performance decline. They have made accommodations, but her performance is still not up to par. There's urgency for her to come to terms with her situation before she starts seeing subtle signs of being pushed out of her job.

Both Jose and Jack present situations that require intensive adjustments if they are to continue working. In fact, there may be questions as to whether it would be best to apply for Social Security Disability benefits. In Jose's situation, these benefits could still allow for part-time work during periods between treatment and recovery, as well as the possible advancement of his illness. Award of Social Security Disability benefits requires an inability to work full-time but does not preclude earning some income.

Jack presents a slightly different situation. His only feasible work option is to try to find ways to use his technology skills to work from home. However, he can't focus and function consistently due to his anxiety. He needs continued treatment and vocational rehabilitation, which he can get from the Department of Veterans Affairs (VA). However, these things take time and the results are unpredictable. Since he has medical evidence to show he can't work, he may also want to apply for Social Security Disability benefits and/or a higher amount of VA compensation to help with income.

Maintaining Self-Worth

For those of us entrenched in a career, we find ourselves wanting to continue using our skills and making meaningful contributions, despite our health limitations. An inability to do so can have a profound impact on the worth we attach to ourselves, and on our self-identity.

Fortunately, there are usually alternative directions to allow work to continue. It may be modification of the job environment or how we do our current job, part-time employment, or even sporadic work in combination with Social Security disability and/or disability payments through worker's compensation, VA disability compensation, or long-term disability insurance. There are instances, however, when it's necessary to take the total disability route if it's available, leave work behind, and embark on a new path of life satisfaction.

If you are looking at a potential career transition due to reduced functional capability, whether it's a minor change or a decision to seek disability benefits, it's often worthwhile to confidentially explore your feelings, consider the options, and take steps toward transition with the guidance of a qualified rehabilitation counselor or consultant. Rehabilitation counselors are trained, nationally certified, and in some instances, state-licensed to specifically help clients with disabilities deal with work-related issues. You can get the name of a certified rehabilitation counselor in your area through the Commission on Rehabilitation Counselor Certification directory (https://tinyurl.com/ybhod9wh). Upheavals in mid- or late career often involve emotional ups and downs, and these are best navigated with professional aid and support.

CHAPTER 24
Options When Disability Prevents Full-Time Work[16]

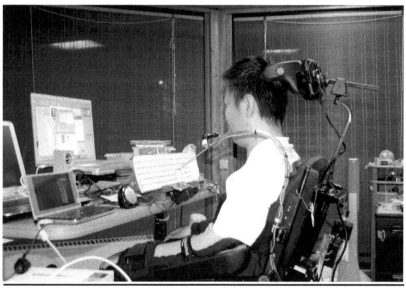

Photo by U.S. Department of Labor

Deborah's Sudden Loss

Deborah, 52 years old, was a lead systems analyst for a regional finance company. She had to leave her job a year ago due to nerve impingement from disc injuries to her neck after an accident at home. Even with surgery and medication, the range of motion in her neck and ability to use her arms is limited, and she now needs to lie down four to five times throughout the day to minimize pain. Her doctor says that she shouldn't work

---

16 This chapter was co-authored by Steven Simon, Ph.D. and Fernando Narvaez, Esq.

more than a total of four hours per day, unless she can work while lying down. She left her job when it became obvious that she could no longer function consistently due to pain.

Deborah is married, with one child in college. Her family has suffered because of her loss of income, even though she eventually managed to find some contract work as an independent consultant, some of which she can do while lying down. Deborah has always gotten great satisfaction from her job. The part-time work has at least continued to provide some sense of achievement in her life, as well as limited income.

> **When illness or disability intervenes in an otherwise meaningful career, it's often important to find ways to preserve and even enhance the possibilities for continued satisfying work.**

Deborah's case is not unique. Many workers are faced with non-work-related illness and disability during their careers, interrupting the ability to work full-time. Obviously, this has financial implications, but for the career-centered professional, the threat of having to stop working prematurely can also unravel the fabric of self-esteem, self-worth, and social status.

In Deborah's case, at work she was seen as the programming guru, the go-to person for the most difficult problems. She has nowhere near that level of status with friends and family. In fact, she's always been viewed as somewhat withdrawn outside of work. Loss of her job status was emotionally devastating at first, despite the serious pain she experiences. That changed to some extent once she started to work part-time. Thus, when illness or disability intervenes in an otherwise meaningful career, it's often important to find ways to preserve and even enhance the possibilities for continued satisfying work.

Disability Benefit Programs

Several potential options exist for dealing with both the financial consequences of leaving a full-time job and the desire to keep working. These include long-term disability insurance policies, Social Security Disability, pension programs that include disability options, tax exemptions or credits, and vocational rehabilitation. Workers' Compensation benefits are also available to most workers who are injured in the course of their employment.

If you have long-term disability insurance and meet the requirements to receive benefits, this can help. Although Deborah had short-term disability benefits from her company, which covered a six-month period, she never purchased a long-term disability policy. Typical policies may cover benefits for two years, five years, or up to age 65. Waiting periods to receive benefits vary and benefits may be 50–70% of earnings subject to a maximum. Such policies may also reduce payment amounts if you get other disability benefits; and may provide only partial payments if you can work some of the time, or if you go to work in a different occupation or for a different employer.

If you are a career professional and become disabled, you might easily overlook Social Security Disability as one of your major financial options. It could be particularly important if you do not have long-term disability benefits and do not have or lose your medical insurance. If you qualify for Social Security Disability, you would receive a monthly allowance as well as Medicare, a substantial additional financial benefit. If you paid into the Social Security system during your work years, you may be entitled to this help.

One of the most common misconceptions about Social Security Disability is that an individual cannot work at all. The rules on employment while receiving Social Security benefits are complex, but generally if you do not exceed the level of what Social Security considers Substantial Gainful Activity (SGA), your benefits will not be affected. In Deborah's case, when she was granted benefits at $1,800 per month, she could still work part-time as a consultant from home as long as her part-time income did not exceed $1,170 per month.

For those who work for a government entity, disability benefits may be available, whether or not contributions were made to Social Security. Benefit criteria and amounts, as well as rules for working while receiving disability benefits, differ based on the plans.

Workers' compensation is available only to those who are injured on the job. Programs differ in each state and provide wage replacement, medical benefits, compensation for economic losses, and vocational rehabilitation benefits that will presumably result in return to work.

There are also some tax credit programs that can increase income by lowering taxes. Homestead exemptions exist in many states and counties for permanently disabled homeowners. The Earned Income Tax Credit (EITC) for use on your federal tax return may also be an option, particularly, like Deborah, if you have some earned income or file jointly with a spouse who has earned income.

Return to Work Options

In Deborah's case, she had the skills and background to continue her career doing contract work, even though it was only part time. This was a great alternative for her, since it keeps her actively pursuing the career she loves and helps her to maintain some of the status she lost. She was able to find a work arrangement that provided the flexibility to adjust to her medical needs and to expand the work she accepted based on her physical capacities during recovery. Also on the positive side, it created the opportunity to develop her own business, a transition that she had always thought about.

If Deborah's accident had been job-related, she would have had workers' compensation benefits to assist with returning to a work alternative, in addition to paying medical costs. When workers' compensation benefits do not apply and other help is needed with return to work, government-supported vocational rehabilitation benefits may be available to provide evaluation, counseling, medical and supportive services, equipment, training, and education to qualify for a new career, as well as for job placement help. The purpose is to prepare and help you find a job or new career that you can do full- or part-time within the constraints of your disability.

The major vocational rehabilitation program in the U.S. is the State-Federal program operated in each state through the Division of

Vocational Rehabilitation or a similar state agency. Such programs usually have numerous local offices. Due to budget constraints, most states have an established order of selection and some have financial tests before they can provide full services. Usually the order of selection favors applicants with the most serious disabilities. Although the services can be extensive to even include diagnostics and treatment to eliminate employment impediments, it's worthwhile to inquire further or apply directly for services in your state to determine the extent of services you can expect. To find a state program visit PARC (https://tinyurl.com/6ondkkx).

The U.S. Department of Veterans Affairs (VA) also operates a comprehensive vocational rehabilitation program for service-disabled veterans. Once eligibility and entitlement are established, all needed services can be provided without order of selection or financial tests. Each VA Regional Office has one or more Vocational Rehabilitation and Employment (VR&E) offices throughout its covered area and every state has at least one VA Regional Office. To find your area visit U.S. Department of Veterans Affairs (https://tinyurl.com/yaubw9vw).

In summary, if you must stop working full-time, all is not lost. There are usually financial options to help keep you afloat and employment options that can be tailored to create a fulfilling work situation despite your limitations.

CHAPTER 25

Social Security Disability[17]

It's Not Just the Money

In chapter 24, we discussed general options available to maintain income and meaningful career activities, even if you are no longer able to work full-time. In this chapter, we focus specifically on Social Security disability, a powerful tool, particularly if you are a professional with a career-impacting disability who can and wants to continue to do some work.

To summarize our case study, Deborah, a 52-year-old systems analyst, had to leave her full-time job a year ago due to the effects of a neck injury from a fall at home. Her doctor said that she could work no more than four hours per day unless she could work lying

---

17 This chapter was co-authored by Steven Simon, Ph.D. and Fernando Narvaez, Esq

down. After leaving her job, she received short-term disability for six months, but after that the loss of full-time income placed a severe financial burden on her family, even though she was able to do a little part-time consulting work.

Deborah was very involved in her career, and the inability to go to work any longer caused her loss of status and self-esteem, with resulting depression. Her part-time consulting work has begun to restore her career involvement, status, and positive feelings about her future, as well as adding a little family income.

Like most people her age, Deborah never expected to become disabled. She knew she could be eligible for Social Security retirement at 62, but she didn't know anything about the substantial benefits that could be available to her now through Social Security Disability. This would include monthly payments, as well as Medicare. The latter is critical, since her family policy under the Affordable Care Act is costly and has high deductibles. This could worsen with any changes to the health care laws.

With her new medical costs, Deborah could potentially face bankruptcy in the future. In addition, if she qualified for Social Security disability, Deborah could still work part-time, which would allow her the opportunity to not only better meet her financial needs, but also to at least partly continue her career.

Eligibility

To be eligible for Social Security disability, you must be "insured" by virtue of having paid into the Social Security system during prior employment. For each year that you worked and paid into the system, you accumulate a number of credits, up to four per year. Depending on your lifetime earnings, you can establish whether or not you are insured. You can check online to see if you've acquired sufficient credits by creating a free account through the Social Security website (http://www.ssa.gov/myaccount/). The account allows you to see your entire Social Security history.

Social Security will take into consideration your age, education, and prior work experience. Based on these factors, you must then be able to establish through medical evidence that you are unable to work, or sustain employment, with whatever remaining physical and mental capacities you have. Therefore, it is very important that your treating physicians are aware of limitations such as having to lie down during the day to relieve pain (as in Deborah's case), having to take multiple rest periods due to fatigue, side effects of medications, headaches, and any other symptoms that preclude you from completing a full workday or work week.

Benefits and Incentives

—

Social Security provides various incentives to assist individuals in finding opportunities to return to part- or full-time employment.

—

If you are granted benefits, the average monthly payment was $1,172 in September 2017(https://tinyurl.com/jtzc2sy), but can go as high as $2,687, and is based on a formula using your averaged indexed monthly earnings and primary insurance amount.

The rules on working while receiving benefits are somewhat complex. Generally, if you do not exceed income in any month of what Social Security considers Substantial Gainful Activity-$1220, or $1240 if blind, for 2019 (https://tinyurl.com/j72cuy4)—your benefits will not be affected.

As an example, if Deborah was granted benefits of $1,800 per month, she could still work part-time as a consultant from home as long as her part-time income did not exceed $1,170 per month.

If you are concerned about maintaining your career, you will probably want to return to work part time as Deborah did, or eventually full-time, if at all possible. Social Security provides various incentives to assist individuals in finding opportunities to return to part- or full-time employment. The "Ticket-to-Work" program provides disability recipients with various tools to transition back to the workforce without losing their disability benefits, including assistance in finding a job. This information is available at Ticket To Work (www.chooseworkttw.net).

Also, Social Security disability provides recipients with a "trial work period" in which you may test your ability to work for at least nine months without losing your benefits. The nine months do not have to be consecutive as long as they are within a 60-month period.

During this trial work period, you may continue to receive full disability benefits, including Medicare, regardless of how much is earned, as long as the work activity has been reported and the medical impairments continue. This provides a good opportunity to test out your capacity for full-time work without the threat of losing benefits if you cannot do so. Certain other rules may apply, and disability recipients should contact their local office first.

The full criteria for being granted Social Security disability benefits are too complex to cover here but are available at Social Security Administration's website (www.ssa.gov/disability). Note, though, that it is important to file for benefits as soon as possible after becoming disabled, since granting of benefits carries a five-month waiting period from the date you are deemed disabled, and the processing time for an initial application can take a few months. In some instances, the process can take even longer.

As you can see, if you are unable to work full-time due to disability and can establish eligibility to receive Social Security disability, multiple benefits are available. You can have the opportunity to fortify your income through monthly benefits, have the financial savings of Medicare (vs. high cost medical insurance or self-pay) and the ability to take care of all your medical needs, plus you can still pursue your professional career.

CHAPTER 26

Resuming a Career with Illness or Disability[18]

Photo by kaboompics

In chapters 24 and 25, we discussed financial options to replace income and provide medical services if you can no longer work full-time due to disability, as well as some options for returning

---

[18] This chapter was co-authored by Steven Simon, Ph.D. and Fernando Narvaez, Esq.

to work. This chapter expands further on how you can continue your career on a more limited or eventually a full-time basis dictated by the work capacity you still have.

In the prior chapters, we used Deborah as our example. After becoming disabled and leaving her full-time systems analyst job, she was able to do part-time consulting work from home. She also was granted Social Security disability benefits which allowed her to make up to $1170 per month without losing any of her disability benefits.

Working at Home

So, what are some ways of getting and doing work in these types of situations? In Deborah's case, as a contractor, in effect, she started her own business. She had some contacts at her former company, one of whom was able to assign her short-term contract work. She also used her LinkedIn and Facebook profiles to make her skills and her desire to contract known. This brought her more opportunities to bid for work, some of which she got. Since she could work at home, she was able to set up her computer to do most of her work in a more comfortable, partially prone position. Although her projects had deadlines, she had the flexibility to arrange her work during times when her pain was less.

The ability to work at home offers great advantages, as in Deborah's case. If you are already self-employed, such as an accountant or an attorney, much of your work could be transferable to a specially arranged home setting with assistive devices or software, if necessary.

With data and files storage capability now easily available through the "cloud," and communication availability through phone and video, going to an office is not necessary for many tasks. In fact, virtual office services such as phone answering, call switching to virtual numbers, and video meeting capabilities can make running a business from home as routine as working from an office.

If you do not already have a business, home businesses can be developed on internet venues, such as eBay, or directly through social media. For example, a client developed a specialized food sales business strictly using Facebook. She was able to do this at home, accommodating for her disability limitations. Although she was granted Social Security disability for the period she could not work productively, she ultimately made enough income that she no longer needed disability benefits.

If you are not entrepreneurial, are not oriented toward self-marketing, or your skills or occupation are not well-positioned to developing a business, there are other options for working part-time at home. Most offer the opportunity to work in a postural position that suits you if you have physical limitations. If your ability to focus and concentrate is impaired at times or you have other mental limitations, some home jobs, particularly project work, also allow for flexibility in when you do the work.

There are several legitimate websites that offer or advertise jobs that can be done at home. Legitimacy is an issue because there are many ads online for part-time work at home that may not deliver or may require the user to pay a fee. We strongly suggest avoiding those. The following is a listing of reliable sites:

www.workingsolutions.com/

www.liveops.com/

www.guru.com/

www.topconsumerreviews.com/

www.alpineaccess.com/index.php/

https://www.upwork.com/i/how-it-works/freelancer/

Some of these sites allow for bidding on freelance consulting opportunities in a variety of fields. Others provide home-based customer service jobs. Many will require technical or administrative skills or specialized knowledge.

LinkedIn now also offers ProFinder (https://tinyurl.com/y7p7qknf), a marketplace for project work. When you sign up for specified areas of work, you can be notified by email of available projects on which you can bid. Depending upon your areas of expertise, you may get bid opportunities on dozens of projects daily.

For some home jobs, and for most home businesses, you will need to have certain equipment to carry out the work. For example, you will need a computer with an up-to-date operating system, reliable high-speed internet service, dedicated faxing and copying capability, antivirus/malware software on your computer, and possibly cloud-based storage capability.

In some instances, employers will accommodate extended illness or disability with home-based work. A client, Alan, was a data management specialist for a mid-size brokerage firm. When he became ill with metastatic cancer, he needed to spend time away from work for exams, treatment, and recovery. However, his skills were unique, and his employer accommodated by allowing Alan to work mostly at home on his own hours. This

Although being unable to work full-time due to disability can be an unwelcome and distressing situation, the required changes in lifestyle also bring new possibilities for personal and career growth, and even survival.

continued over a 2-year period until Alan's condition deteriorated to the point he could no longer work. He always expressed that the ability to continue in his job maintained his positive attitude and was contributing to his survival. If you are considered a valuable employee in a company, particularly one that is known to make accommodations to employee needs, it's worthwhile to explore the possibilities before deciding to "throw in the towel" and resign.

Non-Home Employer Accommodations

All adjustments to an illness or disability do not require working at home. For example, Ahmed, 44, a recently retired Army major, has bipolar disorder with periods of depression, when he cannot focus or easily leave home. He receives VA compensation payments, since the disability is service-connected, but not enough to fully support himself. Although he has a college degree and a good military service record in the intelligence area, when he got a civilian job, he found it impossible to go to work consistently during days when he was severely depressed. He eventually lost the job.

Ahmed can speak several foreign languages, including Arabic, Bosnian, Croatian, Serbian, and Spanish. As a result, his translating skills are in demand. He also finds translating very meaningful and useful to others when he can use his skills.

He was told by a translating service that if he becomes properly certified, they will hire him to do brief assignments for court systems and in the health care area when he chooses to accept them. This is an ideal part-time opportunity for him, which could involve in-person or telephone assignments when he is able to handle them. If he is in a period of serious depression, he can decline assignments. Since he has a service-connected disability, he could qualify for VA vocational rehabilitation and receive a subsistence allowance and payment for the costs of getting his certifications.

Although being unable to work full-time due to disability can be an unwelcome and distressing situation, the required changes in lifestyle also bring new possibilities for personal and career growth, and even survival. As we have discussed in these chapters, even with severe disability, financial security, continued or new career satisfaction, and even better medical care may well be within reach.

If you have a disability and need help in figuring out how to use your skills and background in doing some level of work within the constraints of your limitations, consider working with a rehabilitation counselor. Sometimes it helps to have a partner with whom you can discuss creative possibilities. Public agency and private sources of receiving vocational rehabilitation help are discussed in chapters 23 and 24.

Photo by Geralt

PART 8

Meaningful Work as Part of Retirement

Continuing to do meaningful work after retirement can have significant benefits. Aside from adding income, if the work is paid, there can also be benefits to your health. Research appears to support that continuing to work, whether full- or part-time, after retirement, particularly in work related to a prior career, is associated with better physical and mental health. Working after retirement may also increase life span (https://tinyurl.com/yd6m877s).

This makes sense. After all, retirement is often seen as a time to enjoy a new phase of life. Why shouldn't enjoyment carry over from the best aspects of work that you've always experienced? Why not continue to use the skills and interests you may have taken decades to develop and which have given you satisfaction in the past?

In retirement, you may also have more flexibility in when, where, and how you use them. In fact, leaving work without at least a transition period of some work can result in a sense of loss and depression unless you have a long-term plan that effectively replaces the time, social status, and job satisfactions work provided in your life.

Even if retiring temporarily feels good and reduces stress, there is still a void that will need to be filled. The time to plan for other activities that will be of enjoyment and interest, including new, meaningful work opportunities, is before the emotional impact of the void takes place. Ideally, this planning should be part of retirement preparation.

CHAPTER 27
Transitioning to Retirement: It's Not That Simple

Photo by Geralt

What You May Be Thinking

If you are on the cusp of retiring, you may be trying to decide what to do about future work. You may have had a lengthy career and are not sure how you will adjust to not working. Although everyone tells you how great it will be to retire, and you've been counting the days, you have some lingering concerns. In fact, you may not be saying much about that to anyone either, not wanting to sound foolish. Deep down you know that as a worker you've had a place to go every day, you have relationships with colleagues, you've made meaningful social and business or professional contributions, and you may have a legacy of achievements to preserve.

Also, your social identity may be deeply rooted in your work. People address you as Mr./Mrs., Ms., Dr., Judge, or Captain, and treat you with the respect that your work status or position demands. When you retire, that may evaporate, except in your immediate social circle. When I counseled recently retired military officers who were used to being viewed and addressed by rank during their careers, it was often difficult to adjust to a civilian world where military status was unknown or irrelevant. If you're in a respected professional or leadership role in an organization, the situation can be similar when you retire and establish a new social circle.

On the other hand, you may have just retired, and are thinking how liberating this will be after leaving the constant stress of your job behind. Then, after a blissful month or two of being away from the work routine or after some travel, recreation, or volunteering, you are getting a little antsy, wondering whether there is a way you can return to some type of paid work, even part-time. Maybe you could use the

> **There are employers who are eager to benefit from the maturity and skills that retired workers can bring.**

money, or perhaps you miss the interactions with some of your colleagues and friends. Or maybe you want to get out of the house and feel more useful or have the satisfaction of still using your skills.

If you are one of those who wants to consider post-retirement employment, you may be wondering about how to approach this new challenge. You may wonder what kinds of part-time or even full-time jobs might be readily available to you as an older worker. You may be afraid that you will be discriminated against because of your age.

Fortunately, there are jobs with part-time or project-based options that are readily available to seasoned workers. Similarly, there are employers who are eager to benefit from the maturity and skills that retired workers can bring.

The purpose and expectations of a post-retirement job are often different for those who have already experienced the grind of advancing in a career, and in some cases, have the bulk of wealth and benefits they need. For example, over the years, some of my best employees have been part-time retired career counselors. What I found is that these highly-experienced professionals simply wanted to do their job and help people. This is why they were in the profession. But, like many late career workers, they didn't have that luxury earlier in their careers when there was a focus on career advancement, money, and dealing with workplace dissatisfaction. And as an employer, I found these retired workers to require less maintenance and supervision with these issues than younger workers. Thus, the costs of supervision were less.

Common Issues Regarding Post-Retirement Employment

There are many issues in getting employed after retirement. What type of work do you want to do? Should it be an extension of what you've done before, or something that fulfills a dream you could never pursue before? Do you have realistic expectations?

If your expectations are too high, you will get discouraged quickly. Charles, a human resources division chief at a federal agency was planning for retirement. He told me that after retirement he could easily get a job in the private sector doing the same thing, and planned to do so. Although he had high status and experience in his agency, his experience in the federal government would have little relevance to running a human resources program in a private company. In fact, longtime career experience only in government might be a liability. So, his thinking, influenced by his government status, was unrealistic. His goal did not materialize, and instead he became a car salesman.

Allison was a finance chief in a local branch of a state agency. As she approached retirement, she told me, "I plan to get a job teaching at the junior college." She had a bachelor's degree in accounting, but no advanced degree. Was this realistic? Although she had a responsible job and her agency thought well of her, she overestimated her value in the job market. In her area, there was no chance for a faculty job unless she was well-known in her field (outside her agency), had something very unique to offer, or had an influential contact inside the department in which she wanted to teach. She had none of these. Even if one has been very successful in their job in a single setting, it's important to temper the tendency to assume experience can transfer to other settings without thorough job exploration.

Other issues include whether you want to work part-time or full-time, whether you want sporadic work or online work so you can mix it with travel, and whether you prefer to work solo at home or go to an office. To help with setting realistic job goals and guiding you through the job search process, it's often a good idea to talk with an experienced career consultant or counselor. This is particularly helpful in avoiding time-wasting mistakes and discouragement if you have not been in the job-search market recently. Discouragement can be highly destructive and can result in giving up on the opportunity to find a significant channel for fulfillment during the retirement years.

So, what are some jobs more readily available to retirees, particularly those with professional or technical skills, and who want part-time, sporadic, or even full-time options? There are a wide range of possibilities that may fit your needs, and resources to help. Chapter 28 delves into this.

CHAPTER 28

Getting the Right Retirement Job

What Are Your Options?

Since this book is about renewal, that is, finding passion for and meaning in work, let's extend that concept into retirement. If you look at retirement as a new, enriching phase of your life, any work that you do should enhance that experience. How do you assess your options from that perspective?

First, remember that the intersection principle proposes four components required to intersect for you to find passion and meaning in work: your best skills, interests, best-fit environment, and job opportunities. In retirement, the ideal is to be able to go back to work, at least part-time, in a past job that meets those conditions, while minimizing the work stressors that you experienced during

your career. Many profes-
sionals, such as teachers,
lawyers, counselors, government workers, physicians,
nurses, and college faculty
members can do this with a
former employer, by finding
a job elsewhere, working as
an independent consultant,
or through self-employment.

If you cannot return to your
former field of work, or
you want to do something
different, you can do other

If you look at retirement as a new, enriching phase of your life, any work that you do should enhance that experience.

paid or volunteer work. Although some further education or training may be required, as for any career change, you also may be able
to directly use transferable skills. Here is a list of jobs to consider,
the skills required, and ideas on where to find them:

1. Online Juror
   Skills/Knowledge: Analytic decision making
   Where to Look: www.ejury.com; www.onlineverdict.com

2. Home Health Care
   Examples: Companion; Patient Advocate; Certified Nursing
   Assistant (CNA)
   Skills/Knowledge: Listening attentively; assisting elderly and
   people with disabilities with activities of daily living; interact-
   ing with medical personnel; assisting with medical needs
   Where to Look: Home health agencies; local newspaper ads;
   online listings on job boards and company websites

3. Teaching
   Examples: Teacher; Substitute Teacher; Teacher Aide; Tutor;
   Adjunct College Faculty Member
   Skills/Knowledge: Teaching; small group management; subject
   matter expertise; required education and training, license or
   certification
   Where to Look: Local public and private schools; teaching abroad possibilities (https://www.goabroad.com/
   teach-abroad)

4. Sales
   Examples: Telemarketer; Retail Salesperson
   Skills/Knowledge: Selling; customer service; knowledge of specific products
   Where to Look: Find and approach local businesses directly; online listings on job boards and company websites

5. Online Product Sales
   Skills/Knowledge: Business development; business management; knowledge of internet selling and sales channels (e.g., eBay, Amazon); knowledge of internet marketing
   Where to Look: Self-employment

6. Home Based Customer Service Representative
   Skills/Knowledge: Customer service; giving and receiving complex information; clear oral phone communications; problem resolution
   Where to Look: https://tinyurl.com/y8qygze8

7. Tour Guide or Docent (Paid)
   Skills/Knowledge: Teaching and explaining clearly; interacting with groups and individuals; customer service
   Where to Look: Tour companies; professional sports stadiums; tour guides abroad (https://tinyurl.com/y7paorak)

8. Library Assistant
   Skills/Knowledge: Customer service; filing; basic use of computer
   Where to Look: Local public libraries; colleges and universities

9. Consulting/Freelance Work
   Examples: Information technology; website design; technical writing and blogging; content writing
   Skills/Knowledge: Varies by specialty
   Where to Look: https://www.upwork.com/i/job-categories/

10. Bookkeeper; Tax Preparer
    Skills/Knowledge: Accounting; bookkeeping; knowledge of bookkeeping or tax preparation software
    Where to Look: Local small businesses; national tax preparing services

11. Research Assistant
    Skills/Knowledge: Use of online library resources for academic
    or business research; knowledge of writing and publication
    styles and procedures for specific disciplines; knowledge of
    research methodology; academic or business writing
    Where to Look: Local college and university departments

12. Medical Transcriber; Medical Coder
    Skills/Knowledge: Medical transcribing; medical coding
    Where to Look: Medquist.com (click on careers);
    https://tinyurl.com/7odpmla (medical coding jobs); www
    .mtjobs.com/ (medical transcription jobs); https://www
    .retiredbrains.com/medical-transcription.html (medical
    transcription jobs)

13. Law Enforcement Worker
    Examples: Security Guard, Loss Prevention Specialist; Private
    Investigator
    Skills/Knowledge: Knowledge of security procedures; com-
    puter literacy
    Where to Look: Private security companies; large depart-
    ment stores

14. Handyman/House Repairer
    Skills/Knowledge: Household repair and remodeling
    Where to Look: Self-employment

Landing the Right Retirement Job

How can you get these jobs? First, you should have a resume that
summarizes your pertinent background and skills. If you haven't
written a resume in a long time, Chapter 14 explains how you
can do that.

If the job involves self-employment and you have no prior experience in running a business, personal assistance and training
courses through SCORE, a partner of the U.S. Small Business
Administration (SBA), offers high-quality mentoring and business
development workshops in most parts of the country. Other local
free community services, often partnering with SCORE and SBA,
can be found through an internet search targeting your area or a
nearby city.

For jobs that can be done from home, reliable websites have been recommended in the above list. For many of the other jobs, you may not see ads posted online or elsewhere. If you have contacts who can help you get the job you want, that's great. However, in most instances that probably won't be the case.

If you know what you want, use the targeting strategies in Part 4 of this book.

AARP (https://tinyurl.com/yd6uuhgb) also offers useful job finding resources and services for employment during retirement. These include a listing of employers (https://tinyurl.com/ya8n6vyc) who have committed to hiring a multigenerational workforce. This may be helpful in targeting during a job search, as well as in using the AARP job search board (https://jobs.aarp.org/v). Retired Brains (https://tinyurl.com/ya25xsvf) also has useful resources.

Important and meaningful work can also be done through volunteer jobs. Many of these are community service related and can use your special skills and interests. Volunteer Match (https://www.volunteermatch.org) can help pinpoint opportunities to explore in your area.

Jobs and volunteer opportunities are also available that do not require unique skills. If you enjoy the activities and you work in a satisfying environment, you can still find meaning and fulfillment. Examples include limo, shuttle, and school bus driving; ushering, greeting, and other guest services jobs at baseball or football stadiums; greeter jobs at retail stores; and jobs in specialized places like national parks. Explore possibilities at www.coolworks.com.

If you'd like to work while vacationing or traveling, consider "workamping," which involves traveling the country while working. You can find out more about such job opportunities at Workamper (https://tinyurl.com/y9a8kbna).

Adding work to your retirement life can provide another outlet for renewal and enhance your experience. Whether you want to work for the added income, for the joy of it, or both, lots of opportunities to fit meaningful work into a retirement plan are there.

PART 9

Recognizing and Managing Emotional Dysfunction at Work

It's quite common for emotional issues to interfere with working effectively and with satisfaction. Some of these intrusions originate from job stressors, while others are generated by the emotional states and disorders that are brought to the job; or some interaction of both.

Emotional dysfunctions can seriously contribute to poor performance and all manner of problems with managers, co-workers and customers. Unfortunately, these are the most difficult problems to correct because they are often observed by others, but not recognized by the person experiencing them as the cause of work difficulties. The impacts are recognized, like bad relationships, angry outbursts, or inability to produce up to expectations, but the source of the problems is misread. Blame may be diverted and ways of dealing with the problems becomes disruptive to everyone. Such is the self-protective nature of how the brain works.

The following chapters delve into these sometimes very difficult issues for employers and employees to confront and how to attempt to recognize and manage them.

CHAPTER 29

Stress, Anxiety, Depression: Chicken or Egg Dilemma

Photo by TheDigitalArtist

The Source—Chicken or Egg?

Many people I speak with about mid-career change are experiencing extreme stress on their jobs, or feelings of anxiety and/or depression. Sometimes the stress is just a result of undue pressure inherent in the job and the anxiety or depression is due to frustration with a career, or indecision about whether to make a change. Other times, there is a long history of emotional distress that impacts on all aspects of life, including at work. So, if you are experiencing stress, anxiety or depression with respect to your job, is that due to a need to change the work you do, where you do it, how you do it, or who you do it with? Or are your difficulties at work caused by the influence of ongoing habits or mental distress which impacts on how you interact in and navigate a work environment and generally approach your life? Is it the chicken or the egg?

What Is Stress, Anxiety and Depression?

First, let's briefly address in practical terms what stress, anxiety and depression are.

Stress at work generally refers to something external that causes a psychological or physiological reaction in you. It could be sexual harassment from your boss, or expectations that you can't meet, or constant hostility from a co-worker. For example, I typically meet with salespeople who are under pressure of having to meet sales quotas that are sometimes unrealistic or unattainable. The stress results in physical and mental symptoms such as stomach upset, loss of sleep, short temper, impatience and so forth. Stress, though, is often transient in that when the stressors are removed, the feelings and other symptoms of stress stop. However, long term or chronic stress can lead to other more serious and ongoing physical and mental problems, such as hypertension, irritable bowel syndrome, increased inflammatory response, as well as chronic anxiety and depression.

Stress can also be self-generated. Diana is a residential property manager. She works day and night and is consistently overwhelmed by her work. She complains of the high stress of her job, yet she also feels that she is not doing enough when she is not overwhelmed. Throughout her career, she has created stressful environments for herself in every job she has had. Stress has become a way of life for her, on and off the job. In Diana's case, stress is a self-generated habit. Without stress, she is not stimulated enough while at the same time the amount of stress she creates makes her feel overwhelmed.

Anxiety involves worry, apprehension, feelings of tension and sometimes physical symptoms such as fast heartbeat, tremors, muscle tension, and rapid breathing. Anxiety occurs when some threat which might be real or imagined is anticipated. For example, at work, you could be always worried about being fired. I lost a job when I was a teenager, a traumatic experience, and ever since, I always had a little underlying anxiety about the possibility of being fired from any job I had. In most cases this was an imagined threat rather than real. Anxiety can also be "free floating" where no cause can be identified. Free floating anxiety can impact on all aspects of life.

Depression is a mood characterized by sadness, unhappiness, and sometimes restlessness. This mood can fluctuate normally or be extreme. At the more extreme end there can be deep sadness and pessimism, suicidal thinking, and at the most extreme, suicide attempts. Depression can be transient and in response to specific situations, such as job loss or work dissatisfaction, or it can be ongoing and fluctuating

Is your career or job the main cause of the stress, or is a life pattern of emotional distress the biggest contributor?

for months, years, or most of a lifetime and unrelated to a specific circumstance. Everyone experiences sadness, unhappiness and periodic discouragement, but clinical depression is generally longer lasting and more difficult to shake off than normal mood fluctuations and responses to difficult life situations.

Chicken or Egg and What Can You Do

If you are experiencing stress, anxiety and/or depression, can you identify the source? Moreover, what can you do about it?

If the source can be found mainly in your occupation, job, or where you work, then intervention in one or more of those areas can help. If you are feeling external stress like the salesperson above, then a change in job or occupation could remove the source. Similarly, if you are in a job that requires participating in high pressure press conferences and you have constant anxiety about saying the wrong thing, anxiety reduction alternatives might include changing jobs, getting more training in media relations, and/or seeking treatment for the anxiety.

With regard to depression, let's say you've worked as a computer programmer for 10 years, but never felt comfortable with the technical nature of the work. You've performed adequately in different jobs, but barely so, and not as well as many of your co-workers. You get your greatest satisfactions from volunteer work teaching children with disabilities. Although you make a very good salary, the longer you do programming the worse you feel about yourself and what you are doing. There is an increasing sense of pessimism and unhappiness in your life because of the importance of work to your self-esteem, and always the underlying fear that you will lose your job to someone better. You've reached the stage of feeling depressed most of the time. Serious planning for a potential change of occupation or job would likely best address this problem.

On the other hand, if you have a long history of self-induced stress, anxiety, and depression or alternating moods that contribute to poor job performance; disagreements and anger with co-workers, customers, supervisors on the job and interactions with friends and family; or you are unmotivated or unhappy with many aspects of your life, then changing your job or occupation is not the likely place to target a change. A new job may feel better at first, but you are likely to repeat the same pattern. In this situation, it would be best to find relief from and learn strategies to manage the emotions and behaviors. Mental health counseling or a combination of counseling and medication can be very effective for that. Counseling can also use or direct you to other modalities, such as exercise, diet, mindfulness meditation, and specialized treatment techniques that can be incorporated in an overall treatment plan.

So, if you are experiencing feelings of depression, anxiety, or related emotional distress associated with your career or job, first try to determine which came first, the chicken or the egg. That is, is your career or job the main cause of the stress, or is a life pattern of emotional distress the biggest contributor? In some instances, it can be both, feeding on each other. However, once you have a handle on the causes, you can decide on where to focus your efforts to get back on the right track with your career.

CHAPTER 30

Managing Pervasive Emotional Dysfunction at Work

Photo by tyowprasetyo

Juanita's Decline

Juanita was program manager of an after-school care program for low-income single parents. She had a long history of personal trauma, including abuse from a former spouse and a daring escape after being held hostage. For many years afterwards she was chronically angry, and overwhelmed by anxiety and depression. Despite this, she made good progress under psychiatric care and went on to receive a master's degree in early childhood education. Subsequently she worked as an after-school teacher and then found the program manager job at a community educational services center.

At first, Juanita did well in the job, but she began to have difficulty relating constructively with her staff, the children, and particularly the parents. She would have angry outbursts, scaring the children, and many of the staff felt they were treated disrespectfully. As a result, she had excessive turnover, adding to her already high stress level.

Several parents were so dissatisfied that they removed their children from the program. The agency director liked Juanita and believed she could do the job, but the parents were now pressuring him to replace her. Juanita's anxiety about possibly losing her job increased. In two instances, she was found by staff sitting in the bathroom, crying and shaking. Although she was encouraged to seek psychiatric help, she did not. Finally, to his dismay, the agency director had to terminate her employment.

Recognizing and accepting that emotional problems are causing or seriously contributing to job dysfunction is one of the most difficult things to do. Lack of insight about this is often part of the emotional dysfunction.

Emotional stress at work is something we've all experienced. At the milder end, it can result in transient feelings of tension, anxiety, or depression. It can occur in response to specific situations, like a conflict-laden relationship with a co-worker or manager, or a lower than expected performance evaluation.

However, these seemingly transient issues can become pervasive, chronic stressors, whether because the problems at work get worse or are not resolved, or because of a longer-term pattern of difficulty dealing with stress in many life areas. As with Juanita, sometimes more serious chronic emotional disorders exist that can impact job success and retention over the entire span of work years.

When pervasive emotional issues exist, or become the norm over time, this can have profound impacts on your ability to adjust to any job and other aspects of life. You know this is the case if you've experienced strings of short-term jobs, terminations, or prolonged periods of unemployment related to how you are perceived and perform on jobs.

Typical issues include being viewed as not doing what supervisors or work teams are expecting, having frequent and unresolved conflicts with others, not being viewed as a team player, low productivity, chronically feeling taken advantage of or of being treated unfairly, being unable to concentrate on your work, and chronic unhappiness with jobs. Often you may feel the problems are not your fault.

Sometimes the emotional issues can include inaccurately perceiving people's intentions as unfairly targeting you; anger control issues such as getting into unresolvable arguments or fights; having severe mood swings making your behavior seem unpredictable to others; having emotional "meltdowns" at work; or even, in extreme cases, experiencing auditory or visual hallucinations that keep your attention away from work.

These issues can result in serious problems in getting work done consistently, constructively relating to others, and ultimately in getting excluded socially or alienated from peers and/or managers. Over time they can lead to consequences that compound an already high stress situation, such as reprimands, performance improvement plans that can't be met, being terminated from jobs, and being unable to get hired in new jobs.

Getting Help

Under the right circumstances, jobs and a career can be a source of significant satisfaction and meaning in life. However, pervasive emotional issues can erase any chance for this and, in fact, make work unbearable. Unfortunately, recognizing and accepting that emotional problems are causing or seriously contributing to job dysfunction is one of the most difficult things to do. *Lack of insight about this is often part of the emotional dysfunction.*

In Juanita's case, she clearly had a history of serious emotional problems. However, in this instance she refused to acknowledge she needed help. She thought she'd overcome her prior problems, and it was difficult to admit that she needed help again. Also, she reasoned that her medical insurance was very limited in terms of covered mental health benefits. She assumed that the cost might be prohibitive, or that she might be forced to go to a public agency where staff would know her from her work in the community. The real issue was her inability to acknowledge that a serious problem existed.

Work problems can go on for years and carry over from one job to the next. If you are entrenched in the stress and feel it keeps piling on, the tendency is often to blame others, file multiple complaints and grievances, or give up, allowing the cycle to continue and repeat. In fact, Juanita blamed the parents for her problems.

If it has been suggested or you suspect that some or most of your repeated work dysfunction comes from your attitude and behavior, it would be worthwhile to stop and rethink your career strategy. If you can consider the value of getting professional support and assistance, the earlier, the better, the good news is that interventions such as counseling, medical treatment, and sometimes medications can make it possible to better normalize life and work. The key is recognition, acknowledgment, and willingness to seek help.

Psychiatrists, psychologists, counselors, and social workers can assist. These professionals work as private practitioners, in behavioral health group practices, and at community mental health centers, which can be found through an internet search. Also, dialing the 211 helpline in most areas of the country will connect to helpers who can identify and make referrals to local services, including free or low-cost mental health facilities. In addition, most medical insurance plans now include mental health benefits. As of 2018, policies under the Affordable Care Act (https://tinyurl.com/ybqbvlov) require such coverage to be offered, although availability of services varies geographically.

Can a Change in Job Help?

Sometimes a change in work to a simpler, less demanding career or job can also help restore job stability. In fact, this is what happened with Juanita.

After being fired, she looked for another program manager job, after-school or pre-school teacher job, but was unable to find one. Due to her prior problems, she was unable to get a strong enough reference and many people in this close-knit community had heard about what happened through the "grapevine." This was probably a good thing, because she would likely again have landed in a job that was beyond her emotional capacity.

Desperate for income, Juanita found a job as an eligibility worker at a county government agency in a nearby town. This was a much simpler job that involved interviewing applicants for public assistance and making determinations based on structured legal criteria. The demands of managing complex relationships with staff, students, and parents were gone, yet she still felt she could help others even though it was difficult to stomach the loss in status from her program manager job.

The eligibility work proved meaningful to her. Although her salary was lower, she now also had fully funded medical insurance to pay for private mental health treatment and she was ready to take advantage of it as prevention for potential problems in her new job. With continuing treatment, she might eventually be able to develop the emotional resources to function effectively enough to return to her former occupation.

Career and Job Change Decision Making

Resources for help in dealing with career issues related to disability have been discussed in earlier chapters. However, when it comes to making decisions regarding career and job changes, because judgment and decision making can be affected by emotional dysfunctions, it's worthwhile to reiterate and expand upon that information.

When disability enters the equation, rehabilitation counselors are usually most qualified to help with career and job change decisions. Rehabilitation counseling, testing and other assessment services for the general public are available through your state's Vocational

Rehabilitation Agency (https://tinyurl.com/y8o35otu). That agency may also provide a multitude of other services, including training, if you qualify due to an emotional or other disability. If you are a service-connected disabled veteran and meet eligibility requirements, rehabilitation counseling, testing, other assessment and financial support for training are available through the VA Vocational Rehabilitation and Employment program (https://tinyurl.com/hx59nq3).

Rehabilitation counselors in private practice can provide similar services to help with career and job change decisions. They can be found by consulting the list of nationally certified rehabilitation counselors available through the Commission on Rehabilitation Counselor Certification (https://tinyurl.com/ybhod9wh). Some certified rehabilitation counselors also practice at rehabilitation centers that provide vocational rehabilitation services. You can do an internet search for these facilities locally. Try to locate rehabilitation counselors with at least a master's degree and the Certified Rehabilitation Counselor (CRC) designation. They usually have the background to provide the highest quality career and job change services.

Employer Support and Stigma

If you are currently working or looking for work and have mental health issues, you may be worried about the stigma of disclosure in getting mental health assistance and how it may affect your current or future employment. This is a legitimate concern to consider before talking to an employer or potential employer about your issues or about treatment.

Although there is much greater awareness these days about the occurrence and impact of mental illness in the workplace, as well as legal protections, some employers do not want to deal with the potential fallout. This could include increased supervision, as well as human resources and legal staff time. Thus, such employers may find ways to avoid hiring or retaining those whom they uncover have mental health issues.

Conversely, some employers are quite supportive in understanding and providing opportunities for assistance. It's a sound investment for organizations which recognize the pervasiveness of mental health needs, disclosed or not, and who want to retain otherwise good employees by providing opportunities to maximize work effectiveness and satisfaction throughout the span of a career. Many employers have confidential employee assistance programs which can help directly or through referrals to community resources. These programs also deal with alcohol and substance use/abuse which occur independently or simultaneously with other emotional disorders.

Confidentiality of Mental Health Information

Most medical programs are covered under stringent provisions of federal laws to protect against disclosure of medical, including mental health, information. However, it's important to recognize that no information is 100% secure. In some instances, you could later be asked to disclose your history of mental health problems and treatment, particularly on applications for certain critical jobs and for some occupational licensing requirements. In many instances, this won't be an issue, and regardless of these caveats, it may be far more important to undergo treatment. If requests for disclosure arise later, you can figure out a strategy to deal with them.

Concluding Thoughts

If you recognize the signs of having a serious emotional disorder that is impacting on your job and career, taking quick action can be career-saving. In the over 15,000 work histories I have reviewed, emotional disturbance has contributed significantly to many of the most dysfunctional career patterns, i.e., short-term jobs, career regression or no career progression, intermittent jobs, few jobs over a long span, underemployment, and no employment. Thus, early recognition, treatment, and sometimes rehabilitation counseling can be both a contributor to a more fruitful and satisfying career, as well as a saver of lifelong income.

PART 10
Getting Professional Career Help

Making career decisions and following through with change is particularly difficult in mid-career and beyond. There's often a lot at stake in terms of career or job investment, career progression, financial status and responsibilities, and family factors—much more than when a career is first starting. If you've read this book, hopefully you have a foundation and some resources to help make transitions that will support a sense of passion and meaning in your work.

However, there can be a definite benefit to working through the process with a professional career counselor (or rehabilitation counselor[19] if you also have a disability). It's an opportunity to test out your thinking, explore new possibilities, and to experience a supportive relationship from someone whose job it is to help you find what you are looking for. It can also provide a check against making unwise changes or failing to make changes when they are necessary.

---

[19] Certified Rehabilitation Counselors have qualifications as professional career counselors with specialized training and experience in working with people with disabilities.

CHAPTER 31

The Value of a Professional Career Counselor

Photo by TheDigitalWay

Is It Worth It?

I've often heard people question exactly what a career counselor does and whether there is enough value to invest the time and money for such services. I've been doing this work for many years in different settings and it's a common thought, in the same way that those with emotional issues and family conflicts question whether counseling or therapy could be of any value or worth what it might cost. After all, these helping fields can be vague in terms of what to expect and in outcomes, not exactly like taking an aspirin and feeling the headache disappear.

If you haven't experienced the effects of counseling or therapeutic intervention, it's difficult to imagine that they can be worth the time, effort, and cost. And there still is the stigma around getting professional help to solve personal problems. It's easier to just say "that's not going to help me."

Since I don't see many professional career counselors writing much about value of their services for the consumer, I think it's worthwhile to tackle this "elephant in the room." I believe there is a need to give some perspective to the issues surrounding value and the overall impact that professional counseling can have on an entire career.

Are You Feeling the Pain?

First of all, for many of us, to seek out career help and especially pay for it, there needs to be some pain. That is, you're up against a situation you haven't been able to resolve, and which is really eating at you. Maybe there is serious conflict with your colleagues or supervisors, political or otherwise, that is literally making you physically ill or depressed. You can't resolve the situation, but you feel trapped. Or perhaps you simply are unhappy with the career you chose, or will never make enough money, and just want out. You know there should be something better and you've thought about it forever, but just don't know where to turn. Enough is enough.

Maybe you work endless hours, have no time for family or anything else, get little recognition, but are locked into a salary. You feel that something's got to give but feel powerless to do anything about it. And perhaps you've been looking for a new job for years with no tangible results. You've had to take part-time jobs, have a less than adequate income, and see no light at the end of the tunnel. These are just a few scenarios I've seen, but you get the point. The pain is emotional and/or physical, and you're near your wits' end. You may not even want to admit it, because you may see it as failure on your part, but it's with you every day.

Serious pain is not always the reason for seeking career help. For example, if you are trying to select a first career and can't decide, it may be evident that seeing a counselor or maybe taking some career tests would help solidify a direction. Long term, it's worth the effort. Or maybe you are transitioning out of the military or are trying to go back to work after being a stay-at-home parent for the last 10 years. You really don't know where to start to resume a decent career or job. So, you're open to getting some help.

What about All the Career Self-Help Websites?

You may be thinking, well there are thousands of websites on the internet with career resources. You can just Google an issue and plenty of job sites and other sources for self-help pop up. Good point. But with all these resources available, how do you choose quality services that are going to work best for you? And if your problem is complex, such as the ones I mentioned above, self-help sites may not do the trick.

Finally, self-help sites can require a lot of persistence to get what you really need, and the best ones are complicated. For example, one of the best free occupational resources in the world is the U.S. Department of Labor's Occupational Employment Network (O*NET) (https://www.onetonline.org/). However, it is so comprehensive that it can require intensive time for a new user to figure out how to best find what it can offer. The site is superior in the career exploration it can generate and the results it can provide. As I have found with my own clients, the most persistent and computer savvy individuals who need to make a career choice will gain a lot. Unfortunately, most users need personalized guidance and will give up if they don't have the help.

Finding Value—Who Should Provide the Help and What's It Like?

So let's say you've come to the realization that you need personalized help. What can professional career counseling do for you? What is the real value? Note that by professional career counseling I mean services provided by someone who has advanced education and experience in both counseling and career services. Someone with that background is in a good position to help because of their counseling skills, broad knowledge of career and job resources, and knowledge of techniques to use in choosing and sustaining careers, and in finding jobs.

These professionals differ from those with mainly human resources, job recruiting, job placement, or self-taught job skills backgrounds, who tend to focus on giving advice based mainly on experiences in the specialty which they know, or their unique background. Professional career counselors are not likely to concentrate heavily on telling you what to do.

If you have career issues you may already be getting tons of advice from friends and family, none of which is all that helpful. No one can really solve your problems by just telling you what to do. The most effective career help strategies encourage you to figure that out for yourself . . . with some help, because sometimes you just don't see it on your own. Professional career counselors are most likely to help you set goals to resolve your career issues and guide you toward achieving them.

No one can really solve your problems by just telling you what to do. The most effective career help strategies encourage you to figure that out for yourself . . . with some help.

They may make suggestions or help you change your behaviors and thinking, but you are always in control of your destiny. In effect, the counselor is your non-judgmental partner in moving you toward where you want to be.

Professional counselors are trained to nurture the type of relationship in which you feel comfortable to share your thoughts and feelings, reflect objectively upon your situation, and make your own decisions. How well this is done is critical to your progress. With the right counselor, it may be one of the few times in your life that you can feel free to discuss your real feelings without fear of being judged or being told what is best for you. This can change your whole perspective. The counselor will use his or her expertise in assessment, career counseling theory, and in career- and job-related knowledge to guide you and provide information that helps you get a full picture of your own strengths AND weaknesses, and the full range of options available to resolve your issues.

For example, if you've been searching for a new job for years and are thoroughly discouraged, the counselor will likely help you honestly explore what you have been doing and why you are failing. It may have to do with unrealistic expectations or pressures from others, mismatch of skills with jobs, job search techniques and strategy, or your communication skills and style. Or it may have to do with detailed aspects of the job search process; for example, a weak resume, interview breakdowns, failure to identify the right potential employers, or effectively using social media.

You may have read all the job-search literature and know about all the techniques, but still not see the problem without the opportunity to reflect with a caring, non-critical, career-knowledgeable partner, and ultimately change your perspective. The result for you may range from some minor adjustments to a whole change in perspective and direction.

You may now be thinking, I know some people who've used a career or life coach. How is this different from using a professional career counselor? The difference comes back to education and experience. Coaches come from a variety of backgrounds. There are no current academic requirements or standards for one to become a coach (although there are some certification programs available). Some professional career counselors are skilled in and will include a coaching approach when it best serves their client. However, coaches may not have the counseling skills, career-assessment skills, background in the career decision making process, and career knowledge to apply when those will bring added value for their clients.

This is not to say that you won't benefit from working with someone who does not have the educational and experience background of a professional career counselor. There are many outstanding providers of career and job help who do not have those credentials and who are highly talented in helping their clients get jobs and manage career issues. However, a professional career counselor brings a unique skill set to the table designed to help clients deal with complex problems and to provide the tools to restart or revitalize a career.

Measuring Career Value: It's Not Only What Happens Now

How do we assess the value of professional career counseling to your career? This is not like in a ballgame where you have a score to indicate success, or in medicine where a pill either cures the infection or doesn't. In counseling, we can most easily measure short-term outcomes, i.e., whether you achieved the goals you set for this counseling process. If you started out with a goal of selecting what is likely to be a satisfying career, did you do that? If you didn't, why not? Sometimes goals in counseling can change rapidly as more information becomes available. When that happens measurement of success can seem like a moving target.

What if you're in the middle of your career and left your job out of dissatisfaction? You have a clear alternate job goal in mind, but after two years of looking you're coming up empty-handed. You've gotten close a few times, but the job interviews are not coming frequently. You finally decide to see a career counselor. After you and the counselor meet, the short-term goal may be to first assess reality of the job goal itself and whether it needs to change, or whether something needs to change in the way of preparation.

The results of that assessment may then lead to other goals, such as changing the job search or interviewing technique, learning new communication skills, getting more training, or even pursuing a new career. The longer-term goal, of course, is landing a satisfactory job. This type of counseling could be short term, or it could involve several quick sessions, some individual work on your part, and then follow-up periodic coaching sessions. Even after getting a job, the hope is that what you gained and learned from this experience will boost your career success over the long run. As you can surmise, the future value of using a professional career counselor is complex, not easily quantifiable, and dependent upon several key factors:

1. The nature of your issues,
2. The quality of the relationship developed between you and your counselor,
3. The commitment you have to the process,

4. Your readiness to persist—do what is necessary,
5. Your willingness to make changes over time.

The counselor can become the catalyst for a chain reaction. If you have been struggling with something that has as much potential future value as your career, the investment and the cost may be worth it. This is not unlike the decision to use a financial planner to help maximize your future financial worth.

Costs and Service Options

So, what about the cost of career counseling? It can range from nothing to exorbitant, and, the quality of the experience may have little to do with price. If your resources for help are non-existent, you can see a counselor at the local state employment office; if you are a college student, you can take advantage of the services of a counselor at the career center. If you have a disability and need career help, you can go to the state vocational rehabilitation services office. If you are a veteran or disabled veteran, you can take advantage of career or vocational rehabilitation services through the closest Department of Veterans Affairs Regional Office.

However, all free services can have their drawbacks. First, make sure you are seeing a professional career counselor, i.e., one who has at least a master's degree and experience in both counseling and career services, who can work to solve the issues you have. Staff qualification standards differ at different organizations. Second, be prepared to run into issues of wait times for services, particularly if you are dealing with a public agency. Third, in most instances, you will need to go to a brick and mortar location for services which may not be close to home, particularly if you live in a rural area. Other options include the use of paid services, through private practitioners with local offices, local or national companies which provide career services, or through distance services that use email, phone, and video. Research shows that distance services can be as effective as or more effective, less expensive, and much more convenient than face-to-face counseling. To find a private practitioner, including those that provide distance services, check the resources in the following section. For specifically finding distance service providers, carefully read the profiles of providers to make sure they are competent and experienced in this modality as well as in career counseling. Other potential resources for distance services include the National Directory of Online Counselors (https://tinyurl.com/y9xg9wvq) as well as some college and university career services programs.

Fees for paid services may range from as low as around $50 per session to packages costing thousands of dollars. Again, high costs do not mean more effective services. Be cautious about high-cost providers promising great results, and steer clear of anyone who guarantees results.

Choosing the Right Counselor

Since it may be difficult to identify a provider who has the requisite qualifications in both counseling and career services, you can check the directory on the website of the National Career Development Association (https://tinyurl.com/yd5qwelc) for qualified providers in your location. Note that those who practice in more than one state may only be listed in the state of their primary residence.

Also, if you have mental health issues overlapping with your career counseling needs, the provider you select should be a licensed professional counselor, licensed mental health counselor, or similarly titled counselor in the state in which you will be receiving those services. For example, if you are experiencing depression that you think needs to be addressed, find a licensed professional counselor in your state who is also a specialist on the career side. The "Find a Therapist" directory (https://tinyurl.com/m6uat8d) on the Psychology Today website can be helpful in this regard. Note that fees for mental health services may be covered by your insurance.

Finally, if you have one or more disabilities or medical conditions that may require a change in job or career, a provider with credentials as a certified rehabilitation counselor would be appropriate. Rehabilitation counselors are also often licensed professional counselors or licensed mental health counselors. Such counselors are qualified to help with career choice, mental health, and disability. The best place to start looking for such a provider is through the listing of certified rehabilitation counselors on the Commission on Rehabilitation Counselor Certification website at https://tinyurl.com/ybhod9wh.

The Bottom Line: Leveraging Future Career Value

So, is there value for you in professional career counseling? Consider it carefully. A small current investment could result in leveraging a great deal of future value in career fulfillment, stress reduction, life satisfaction, self-esteem, and financial gain.

Word-of-mouth is crucial for any author to succeed. If you enjoyed the book, please leave a review on Amazon. Even just a sentence or two would make all the difference and would be very much appreciated: https://www.amazon.com/dp/B07KJG5D8T.

Skills Inventory Worksheets

Part I – List of Skills

For each category, list skills that are still usable without further training, or with limited refresher training.

Skills Learned through Jobs

Skills Learned through Education or Training—also include skills that you will have soon after completing in-process education or training.

Skills Learned through Hobbies, Volunteer work, Home Projects, Community Work, Leadership Activities etc.

Part 2 – Combining skills

Combine and consolidate your detailed skills into a list of no more than 10–15 skills, each as concise as possible with a maximum of 12 words.

Part 3 – Strength of Skills

Rate each of the skills listed in Part 2 on the following scale. Pencil in your rating in the box containing the skill:

1 – One of my worst skills. I do not do this well at all.

2 – I rarely do well at using this skill.

3 – I have about average success in using this skill.

4 – I have good success in using this skill.

5 – I use this skill exceptionally well.

Part 4 – List of Strongest Skills

List only those skills which you rated 4 or 5

Best-Fit Worksheets

Name of Organization:

Instructions: Complete the form in pencil after pre-interview research. Then make corrections after the interviews.

1. For each Component, write in any Aspects of that Component that if present would help you optimize your best skills and interests in this organization's environment. Make reference to details in items 1–7 in chapter 12.

2. After completing 1 above, paying special attention to the Aspects you cited for each Component, check one box a-e representing your level of fit to this organization as follows:

   a. No fit

   b. Limited fit

   c. Adequate

   d. High fit

   e. Close to perfect fit

3. Highlight the three most important Components to you.

4. Consider this a best fit organization if you scored each of the three most important Components in the d or e category, after completing your interview(s).

234 |

Components	Aspects of Components that will support optimizing your best skills and interests	a	b	c	d	e
Similarity of interests to those with whom you would work						
Organization culture						
Team(s) with whom you would work						
Nature and style of supervision						
Industry						
Physical environment						
Company size						
Other - specify						

Best Fit Worksheet Notes

Name of Organization:

| Pre-interview research notes: |
| Questions for interview: |
| Post-interview notes: |

About the Author

STEVEN SIMON, Ph.D. is President, CEO and a career consultant with Human Services Outcomes, Inc. His private practice focuses on mid-career issues of professional and skilled workers.

Dr. Simon has a doctoral degree in counselor education from Kent State University and a master's in rehabilitation counseling from the University of Florida. He has over 45 years of experience as a career counselor; counseling psychologist, supervisory psychologist, and business leader specializing in career and job issues; as a manager of career and job programs for veterans; and as an adjunct graduate school faculty member at Kent State University, The Ohio State University, DePaul University, and the University of South Florida.

He has extensive experience in the workings of large and small organizations at all levels, and in delivery of career and vocational rehabilitation services to veterans. In addition to his private practice, to date Dr. Simon has provided vocational expert testimony in over 15,000 Social Security disability hearings. Most of those cases involved claimants in mid-career and beyond. Dr. Simon is licensed as a professional counselor in several states, is a certified rehabilitation counselor (CRC), is a Board Certified-TeleMental Health Provider (BC-TMH), a Certified Life Care Planner (CLCP), and is a professional member of the National Career Development Association, the American Counseling Association, American Rehabilitation Counseling Association, International Association of Rehabilitation Professionals, and is a Life Status Member of the American Psychological Association.

He can be reached at ssimon@hsoutcomes.com.

INDEX

CPSIA information can be obtained
at www.ICGtesting.com
Printed in the USA
FFHW010905091219
56538503-62393FF

9 781937 801960